Xylophobia

Paperback: 9798344045948

Edited by Anne McGowan and Nathan Trull.
Cover Art by @umermzfr
Layout By Nathan Trull

Printed By Nathan Trull in the USA.

Nathan R. Trull

Contents

Xylophobia

The thuds of a man's footsteps echoed through the deep forest. It was the only sound the man heard. No wind whispered against the trees. No branches tangled or fell. No animals traversed through the trees. There was only silence, other than his footsteps…as well as the quiet, yet powerful footsteps of the creature that chased him.

He could not see the monster, but he knew it was not that far behind him. There was no sunlight, no moonlight, no light at all to guide the man to his escape. The man held up his arms, the one thing he had to prevent himself from running into a tree.

He gasped for air as he tripped over himself. His breaths grew shallow as he felt himself growing too exhausted to keep going. He knew that if whatever were chasing him caught up to him, he would surely be dead. The massive thuds of the creature drew near. Its long, spangly arms slammed against the trees as it used them to propel itself forward.

The man could smell the creature's sickening aura that approached him. It smelled of blood and rotten flesh. As the monster grew closer the man's gasps turned to yelps and he had begun to cry out for anyone to help save him.

The creature had reached him. He could sense it's frightening sense of bloodshed and malice. The creature swiped at the man. He jumped out of the way. His leg was scraped by the creature's sharp claws.

The man picked up a branch and threw it in the direction he sensed the creature from. The creature growled as the man picked himself back up. He continued to run and ignored the massive pain he felt in his leg. As the man desperately looked around for anywhere to escape, something caught his eye.

He saw a glimmering orange light in the distance. No bigger than a bead but close enough that the man dared to reach it. He screamed toward the light and held out his hand while he prayed he could make it to the light.

Chapter 1

The Strange Man

"Are all of you ready?" Hamon gazed upon his fellow venturers to receive an answer.

"Ready as I'll ever be," Lenard sighed as he picked up an empty hiking backpack. He swung the straps across his shoulders. The weight of the bag, even when empty, slanted his stance for a moment before he regained his balance. A testimate to his frailness.

Hamon looked over to the other two venturers, Jarold and Quinton, who both nodded their heads.

"Then let's get moving," Hamon too wrapped an empty backpack around his shoulders and picked up a lantern that was placed on the ground. As he turned his back to leave, a young girl approached him. She had olive hair, with distinct blue eyes that glowed compared to the others brown eyes.

"Can I come too?" She asked with puppy eyes.

"No, not yet" Hamon dismissed. Her smile fell as her head slumped and her shoulders dropped.

Quinton placed his shoulder on Hamon, "Why don't we let Kaylee come. We're just going on a simple food run, I'm sure she could handle that."

"She can come when she's eighteen. We already agreed on that," Hamon said.

"I can't come just this once? I can handle myself, I swear," she clasped her hands together.

"I said no, don't be so eager to rush out there. Stay here and give your mother and father some company while we're gone." Kaylee sighed, then nodded.

"Don't look so sad, there's nothing out there you want to see anyway," Lenard said.

"I just want to see what's out there, I don't care if it's anything at all," she claimed.

Lenard pursed his lips, "Well let me tell you from experience, once you go out once you won't want to leave the camp for the rest of your life." Kaylee crumpled her lips as she crossed her arms.

"Let's get going," Hamon grabbed Lenard's arm as the four of them walked away from their campsite. Their group had recently run low on food. They had to venture out to distant, abandoned camps to find more. It was the same with water. It was obtained by leftover flasks.

Hamon had learned at a young age how essential venturing with others was. Other members provided them with extra pack space, as well as extra eyes to look out for camps. The most important gift other expedition partners provided was comfort, and less fear of the unending darkness that clouded around them.

The one light the venturing group of venturers had was a lantern within Hamon's possession. This source of light only lit up a couple feet around themselves. They left little rocks behind to make a trail to insure they did not get lost. At the campsite, they had their campfires that provided more light. But even with that, not much of this world could be within their view. Hamon kept his ears peeled at all times to make up for this weakness.

Despite the monsters being quite large, they were quiet and would only make noise when it was close to its prey. He needed his members to watch out for even a peep of noise. This is why Hamon and other members instated a no-talking rule when they traveled. They kept completely quiet. Another reason why Hamon did not wish for Kaylee to venture with them.

After hours of searching, the group finally spotted a light in the distance. Another campsite that they were sure to be abandoned. The group took a short hike there. The camp was small, too small to possess enough food for their group. It had one tent and not a single chest laid on the perimeter.

The group gazed upon it and wondered if it was even worth it to search though this camp. "Come on, let's scavenge," Hamon commanded as he waved his hand in a gesture for the others to follow. The group split up to search around the camp for anything to utilize. Lenard and Jarold searched in the tent. Hamon and Quinton searched the grass surrounding the campfire.

"You know…I still think you should have let Kaylee come with us," Quinton argued.

"Why are you so insistent about it?" Hamon asked. He felt safer to talk with the bonfire there to protect them.

"I feel bad for her, she wants to prove herself so much but she can't. I guess I can just relate to that sense of worthlessness," Quinton spun his hand.

"She's still a girl, far too young. I don't even feel entirely comfortable letting her join even when she's eighteen," Hamon leaned on his knee to gaze upon the ground closer.

"How old were you when you started venturing? You had to be much younger than she was," he tapped the back of his fingers on Hamon's shoulder.

"I'm not a role model she should be striving to be like," he said.

"And yet she is, denying that isn't going to make her stop. If anything, it will make her more determined," Quinton said.

Hamon sighed, "So what am I supposed to do? Just let her come on a venture. She could be killed."

"Or she could learn. That's how you got to be so good at venturing."

"Like I said, I'm not a good role model for her, she should be striving to be more like her father," Hamon echoed. Klyde was a far superior role model to him. He was smart, caring and brave, yet kept a cool and collected mind.

"Then how about our next venture, we take her and Klyde with us. It will be us four, the best of the best," Quinton suggested.

"Hate to break it to you but I would consider Lenard to be a better venturer than you," Hamon grinned.

"Pfft, he wishes he was as good as me," Quinton crossed his arms.

"I heard that!" Lenard shouted over. Hamon and Quinton chuckled.

Hamon paused his search as he stepped back and leaned against one of the trees, then sighed, "I'll consider letting her join. But if you're serious about this then I'm assigning you have the responsibility of training her and getting her prepared. No arguments about that."

"That's fine by me," Quinton nodded.

Lenard exited the small tent and approached them, "Oh god…please don't tell me you're actually considering it," he scoffed.

"Find anything Jarold?" Hamon asked as Jarold too exited the camp, ignoring Lenard's statement.

"A couple of MREs, not nearly enough to feed everyone though," Jarold said.

"Anything else?" Hamon asked.

"Yes actually," Jarold pulled out what looked to be a locked wooden chest. Small enough that it could be carried with one hand.

"What is it?" Hamon leaned close toward the small chest to analyze it. It was an oak chest, the wood was dampened and molded from the humid air of *The Forest.* Small splinters cracked along the chest's surface.

"Not sure, it's locked." Jarold attempted to open the top of the chest, only for the latch to be halted by a lock.

"Hmmm, give it here," Hamon held out his arm. Jarold handed it to him. He pulled out a hatchet that he had stored in one of the loops of his jeans, then placed the chest on the ground as he raised the hatchet high in the air. He swung down hard and hit the lock. It snapped in two as the parts flew in separate directions. The recoil budded the front side of the chest in the air for a split second.

Hamon kneeled down as he opened the chest. The group surrounded him to get a look. The inside of it was layered with a red cloth and within was what looked to be some sort of contraption that the venturers had never seen before.

The contraption had what looked to be a wooden handle, plated with iron. Attached perpendicular to the wooden handle was a barrel, with a ring of iron attached to the back end of the barrel and front top of the handle. Hamon carefully grabbed the contraption by the barrel. He held it close to his face as he analyzed it.

"Do any of you know what this thing is?" Hamon asked. The entire group shook their heads.

"Klyde might know, he's seen everything," Quinton stated.

"You might be right about that," Hamon said.

"Look, there's something else in there," Jarold pointed out. Hamon glanced back down at the chest. He now noticed two baggies that must have been covered by the contraption previously.

He carefully pulled out the baggies and scanned it the same way he had done with the contraption previously. One baggie was filled with at least a dozen pellets. The other was filled with a gray powder that the group was unfamiliar with.

"What do you think that is?" Lenard asked.

"I don't know, I've never seen anything like this before," Hamon said.

"What should we do with it?" Quinton questioned.

"We'll keep it for now. Maybe Klyde could tell us what to do with it." Hamon placed all of the items back in the chest. He unwrapped his backpack. He opened the zipper and carefully placed the chest within. "Let's get on with it. Quinton, give me a rundown."

Quinton organized all of the items that were found on the camp. "We've got seven MREs. Two flasks of water, one is half empty, the other is completely full. I would say around the ballpark of a liter and a half of water. We also got a jacket; it doesn't seem to be any of our sizes."

"So, we got nothing," Lenard scoffed as he tapped the palm of his hand on his leg.

"That's fine, we'll find another camp. Anyone need anything to drink or eat before we continue," Hamon waved his hand flat toward each of the members.

"I'm good," Jarold stated.

"Same here," Quinton agreed. Lenard shook his head.

"Alright, then let's get a move on." Hamon placed his backpack on his back again. Lenard packed all of the items in Quinton's bag for him. Just as the group was going to continue, they heard a noise come from the woods.

"What was that?" Hamon shot a gaze in the direction the noise came from. Another noise came from the same direction. This time, it was clear enough to be audible. It was a man that screamed for help.

"Shit, what do we do?" Lenard questioned.

"Stay put, don't panic," he sheathed his hatchet once more. Another scream of help echoed far closer this time.

"We should run for it, get out of here before whatever the hell that is reaches us," Jarold argued.

"If we run we could end up losing each other, just stay still for now." The screaming man's footsteps became audible as well. The group huddled together. They prepared themselves for whatever would reach them. The footsteps grew louder and louder. A man appeared from the darkness. Hamon retracted his hatchet as the man ran straight into him. The two of them fell to the ground.

"Shit!" Jarold yelled out. The three of them reached down to the ground. Lenard and Quinton helped Hamon to his feet. Jarold shoved the man away from the group. The man gasped and sweat profusely.

Hamon positioned himself in the front of the group. "Who are you?" He interrogated the man. The strange man held up his hand and gestured that he was too out of breath to answer right this second.

Hamon gazed upon him. He was a younger fellow, somewhere in his mid-twenties, around ten years younger than himself and had brown spikey hair and green, jaded eyes. He faced the ground with his palms placed on his knees. He glanced up as his breathing slowed and relaxed.

"Sorry for running into you," the man apologized.

"You didn't answer my question, who are you?" Hamon repeated.

"I'll tell you that later. Do any of you have any weapons? A monster was chasing after me and I doubt it has any intention of stopping now," The man claimed.

"You lead a monster to us?" Hamon questioned.

"Not intentionally. I just saw a light and ran to it. Anyway, you didn't answer my question, do any of you have any weapons, quickly now," he said.

The group quickly patted through their possessions. "All I have is this hatchet," Hamon held it out toward the strange man.

"That won't be good enough, even for a normal creature. We need something stronger," The man stated.

"We should run, fighting is just going to get someone killed," Lenard said.

"I tried that, it will catch up to us and kill us before we make it anywhere. I only got lucky that it was preoccupied with other people to have a head start," his breathing slowed to a normal pace.

"What about that contraption we found," Jarold mentioned.

"What contraption?" The man questioned. Hamon looked back at the group. He wasn't sure if he could trust the man enough to give the contraption to him. A roar from the monster could be heard echoing through the forest.

"Shit! Hurry up! Quickly!" The strange man begged. Hamon unwrapped his bag. He opened the zipper and retrieved the chest. He handed it to the man. The man opened the chest.

"You found this? This will work perfectly!" The strange man cheered. Out of the darkness a spangly long black arm swiped at the back of the strange man that launched him toward the ground. The monster came into full view. A sickening creature with long spangly arms, a body of an ape with a humanoid, distorted head. Its teeth were like spikes and its eye voided except for its terrifying, piercing, white eyes.

"Run!!" Hamon commanded. The group turned their backs toward the man as they sprinted from the monster. They ran as fast as they could while making sure to keep in line with Hamon since he was in possession of the lantern.

Before they could make any distance the monster reached them. It swiped down at Lenard. Hamon tackled Lenard as the claw of the monster came crashing toward the ground next to them. The lantern fell out of Hamon's hand and rolled further in the forest. Hamon sheathed his hatchet as the monster retracted its arm.

The monster swung again. Hamon sliced the monster's hand. The monster hissed as he backed away. Its dark green excrements spilled across the grass. It reeked of tar and blood. Hamon stood up. He grabbed Lenard's hand. "Everyone run back!" He shouted. Quinton and Jarold followed his direction.

"Lenard! Hand me the jacket!" Hamon instructed as they were darting toward the campfire. Lenard swung his backpack in front of him as he struggled to get the zipper off.

The darkness made opening the zipper far harder. Hamon saw the monster caught up to them in an instant. He could only see the monster because of the low light from the lantern that laid far away. Its uninjured arm swiped in Lenard's direction. He jumped in the way as he laid another strike against the monster. It howled in pain once more.

Lenard retrieved the jacket and handed it to Hamon. Hamon wrapped the jacked around the metal part of his ax. The group reached the campfire then stood still as they awaited Hamon's instruction. Hamon darted straight to the fire, then placed his ax within. The monster grew closer to them. The dark green liquid that poured from the monster splashed on to the ground after each step it took.

"Hamon, whatever you're doing you better hurry!" Quinton shouted.

"Just wait!" Hamon waited for the cloth to ignite. The monster now became visible. It gave a growl that sent a shiver down their spine. The men shriveled in fear as the monster began to tower over them.

Hamon saw the cloth finally ignite. Just as the monster swung down at the men Hamon jumped in front of them as it held the fire close to the monster.

The monster retracted its arm and stumbled back toward the darkness of the forest. Hamon kept the makeshift torch steady as it growled at him. The torch made the monster cautious to approach. It ignored the fire as it struck him. Hamon was catapulted toward a tree. The rest of the group tripped on to the ground out of fear.

"Run!" Hamon commanded. His voice was muffled from blood pouring from his mouth. The men heard his command but were too struck with fear to move.

"Run!!!" He pleaded, but the men were too fearful. The beast once again towered over them. It raised its arm as it prepared to strike. Lenard looked toward the monster, then closed his eyes.

Then, the strange man stepped in. He pointed the contraption at the face of the monster. A flash of bright light came over as a deafening sound traversed through the forest. Lenard glanced upwards. The monster stood still, then fell limp onto the ground. A hole in its head poured out blood.

"What just happened?" Lenard questioned.

"I'll tell you in a minute, first we should help your friend," The strange man said. Lenard nodded as he stood up. His eyes remained glued to the monster. He feared it could pounce up at any moment to attack.

"Don't worry, it's dead," the man calmed Lenard's fears. Lenard gave him a suspicious glare. He knelt down toward Hamon and wrapped his arm around his shoulder. He hoisted him upward and carried him over to the rest of the group.

"You alright Hamon?" Lenard asked.

"I'm fine, I think the bastard just fractured my rib," Hamon said while he kept his hand rested on his chest.

"That doesn't sound like nothing," a concerned look dawned on Lenard's face.

"I'll live. More importantly, I think it's time you tell us who you are," Hamon demanded the man.

"Fine. My name is Picc. I'm a venturer like you guys," he did not glance at Hamon or Leanrd while he spoke, just kept his eyes on the monster and analyzed it.

"What about that contraption? What is it? How do you know how to use it?" Hamon questioned.

"It's a flintlock pistol, it uses gunpowder to propel a pellet at extremely high speeds. It's a quite effective weapon, likely more effective than any weapon you already have."

"But how do you know that?" Lenard asked.

"It's a long story, we should get somewhere safe before I tell you. Do you men have a campsite anywhere?" He gestured his forearms to the men.

Lenard glanced toward Hamon, "You think we should trust him?"

"He did save our lives," Hamon claimed.

"I don't know..." Lenard expressed visible distrust toward Picc.

"I don't like him either. But he could be useful, he took down a monster with ease," Hamon said.

"I guess you're right..." Lenard uttered.

Hamon nodded, "We live a couple miles from here. If we leave now, we should make it there in a couple hours. But we can't leave right now, we still need to find food for our group."

"Why don't we bring back the monster and eat that?" Picc suggested.

"Are you joking or are you out of your mind?" Lenard interrogated.

Picc gestured his arms out wide, "I'm serious, I've done it before. Although their blood is gross and might be toxic, if we roast the meat before we eat it, that should get all of the toxins out of it. I'll even eat first to ensure you I'm not playing any tricks."

"That might not be a bad idea," Jarold chimed.

"It's out of the question," Lenard stated.

"We'll allow it," Hamon interjected. Lenard quickly glanced at Hamon in confusion. "We don't have many options. Our group *needs* food." Lenard opened his mouth to argue but closed it and said nothing. Without this food that could be in trouble.

"Fine…Quinton, Jarold, you carry it. I'll handle Hamon," Lenard tilted his head toward the monster's corpse. Jarold and Quinton nodded and picked up the monster. Each of them grabbing the other end.

"Follow those two, they'll lead you down the trail. We'll catch up in a bit," Lenard directed Picc. He nodded and followed Jarold and Quinton down the pebble path. Once they were out of distance Lenard began down the path himself.

"So…why did you want to wait?" Hamon questioned.

"I don't know about that guy…I don't like him," Lenard said.

"You just met him. Besides, what else are we supposed to do? We can't just leave him out here on his own," Hamon gestured toward the abyss.

"I know…just keep an eye out for him. I don't like the look in his eyes," Lenard claimed.

Hamon snickered, "What look in his eyes? It's not like you to get all spiritual."

Lenard shook his head, "It's not spiritual. It's practical, there's not a hint of fear in his eyes. Someone like that shouldn't exist, especially if they were traveling on their own."

"He could just be relieved that he found other venturers," Hamon patted Lenard's shoulder as he pushed past him.

"I don't know…I feel that…he's going to be the death of us all," Lenard uttered.

Chapter 2

Ray of Hope

Hamon and Lenard arrived at the campsite soon after Jarold, Quinton and Picc had. When they arrived they noticed everyone crowded around Picc, who was at the center of the campsite. Hamon gazed across the three fires and six tents that comprised their camp. In the center fire, Jarold and Quinton were working together with Picc to rest the monster over the fire in the correct position.

Everyone who surrounded the camp had now noticed Hamon and Lenard standing near the edge. They huddled amongst each other, then Amber and Klyde approached them.

"Are you alright? We heard about the monster attack," Amber asked Hamon as she clung to Klyde's side. She bit her lip as she gazed at Hamon's exhausted figure.

"I'm perfectly fine. The damn thing just swiped my ribs," he said while he clutched his side.

"Why don't I bandage you up?" She asked.

"I'll be fine." Amber responded with a harsh glare. He sighed, "...Fine…"

Lenard laughed as he handed him off to Amber, "Take good care of him."

"You know I will," Amber carried him into one of the nearby tents. Lenard turned his attention to Klyde.

"Are you alright?" Klyde asked.

"Me? I'm fine, I wasn't hit or anything," Lenard waved.

"I know…but…getting hit physically isn't the only way to get hurt, friend." Klyde stated.

He felt a tad of frustration that Klyde would think he would have another freakout. At least, that's what he thought Klyde was suggesting. He had asked the question in a strange manner. It also wasn't like him to dig in personally like that.

"What? No…Hamon was there, you know he would stop me from panicking if he noticed," Lenard said.

"If you say so," Klyde uttered. Lenard turned his gaze to everyone surrounding the main fire. Jean and Kaylee were next to Picc and swarmed him with questions. He couldn't hear what he was saying but could see him displaying the pistol to the girls.

"What did I miss?" Lenard asked as he stepped next to Klyde.

"Not much, Jarold and Quinton got here not too long before you did. You arrived just as Quinton finished explaining everything," Klyde said.

"Great…" Lenard sighed. He hoped Picc's visit would not last too long here. There was something wrong with that guy, he could feel it.

"Are we really going to eat that thing?" Klyde questioned.

"So says this Picc guy. I'm not though," Lenard crumpled his lips. Even if he was on his last legs, he would rather die than eat it.

"I'm going to wait and see him eat it first. I'm just worried Kaylee is going to jump ahead and try it right away," Klyde echoed his sigh.

"You need to keep a leash on that girl. She's going to get herself killed if she keeps acting like that," Lenard pointed to Kaylee.

"I wish I could, but she admires her mother too much," Klyde shook his head in disappointment. Lenard wondered if Amber telling all those stories of the other world was something she regretted doing. Amber wasn't like the rest of them, she was like Jarold. They both happened to appear one day within *The Forest*.

Neither of them remember the exact day that they appeared. When they did appear, memories of the other world slipped away from them like a fleeting dream. They were unable to hold onto those memories efficiently. Amber certainly had a better memory than Jarold.

This led Kaylee to admire her mother. Tales she would tell Kaylee of the other world seeped into her head. Kaylee became obsessed with the idea of making it to this other world. Despite the many warnings her own mother gave to her about this place being unreachable, that didn't tear her interest away at all.

Lenard and Klyde approached the fire with everyone else. Jean noticed them as well and stepped over to them.

"You guys are just in time, Picc is about to try some of the monster meat," Jean cheered.

"I am so unbelievably excited," Lenard sarcastically stated. Jean rolled her eyes. She was another member that shared an interest in *The Forest* like Kaylee. However her interests were still quite different from Kaylee's.

Klyde chuckled, "Seems like you two are already buddies."

"I mean, you have to admit trying monster meat takes some guts. It's respectable," Jean said.

"It's stupid. A guy like him is either going to get himself or other people killed," Lenard claimed.

"Come on…you guys have done your fair share of risky stuff, what's so different about this," Jean gestured her hands toward the center fire.

"I wasn't trying to be risky. No smart person willingly puts themselves in a risky situation," Lenard said. Jean rolled her eyes once more.

"Ignore him, he's just like that," Klyde said.

"Whatever, I'm going back over to ask him more questions." Jean turned her back toward them.

Lenard exhaled, "Man…I don't know how her sister puts up with her." Her bratty attitude was a lot to deal with. He thought she would move past it now that she's eighteen, but she still likes to argue.

"They're just young and curious, it's a phase that will pass soon enough, I'm sure," Klyde said.

Lenard laid his palm in the girl's direction, "Even more reason to be harsh. It gets that curiosity out of them as soon as possible."

"You don't seem to have high regards for dreams and wishes." Klyde chuckled.

Lenard turned to face him, "Don't you feel the same way?"

"Who knows," Klyde shrugged. "There could be mysteries unknown out there, maybe even right under our noses. Like the pistol," he gestured, "I've never seen that before."

Lenard furrowed his brow with a smile, "Really? Something you've never seen before? That's something I've never seen before."

Lenard heard someone emerge from the tent behind him. He turned to find Hamon with Amber following closely behind him. His stomach was wrapped in bandages.

"Oh, you're not dead, how unfortunate," Lenard said.

"Oh, you can still talk, how unfortunate," Hamon grinned. Lenard smiled.

He turned toward Klyde, "What's happening?"

"Nothing much, the new guy's still roasting that beast," Klyde said.

"Did the new guy show you the gun?" Hamon asked.

"Jarold did, he asked me if I knew anything about it," Klyde said.

"Do you?" Hamon arched an eyebrow.

"Not a damn thing. Never seen it before," Klyde shrugged.

"That's surprising to hear coming from you. If that's the case the new guy might have more knowledge than you," Hamon joked.

"Hey now, let's not get too wild with the assumptions," Klyde bragged. The four of them laughed. Amber turned her gaze over to the fire where she witnessed Kaylee seemingly loading the new guy with questions.

"Kaylee! Don't give him so much trouble!" Amber scolded.

Kaylee shouted; "I know!" across the fire.

"That girl, I don't know what I'm going to do with her. She hasn't even come over to welcome you back, has she?" Amber crossed her arms.

"Nope, we're too old for her," Lenard shrugged. He remembered the days when she was little when she would run up to them with glee, cheering their names when they returned. She was so cute back then, he wondered what happened to her.

"Ugh. Kaylee! Get over here!" Amber demanded. Kaylee nodded and made her way to Lenard and Hamon.

"Hey guys," she smiled.

"Kaylee! Greet them with respect." Amber scolded.

"It's fine," Hamon dismissed her with a hand, to which she responded with a displeased groan. "I see you're infatuated with the new guy." Hamon leaned in and hugged Kaylee, who echoed his hug.

"Just like Jean is. You two are doomed," Lenard remarked.

"Whatever, you're just old," she grinned.

"Kaylee! How many times do I have to tell you to treat him with respect!" Amber said.

Lenard smirked, "Yeah kid, listen to your mother. If it weren't for us you wouldn't be eating anything."

"Not for long, this new guy's going to eat the monster meat. We might be eating some real meat soon," Kaylee mentioned.

"Pfft, that guy's going to die five minutes tops after eating that stuff," Lenard waved his hand.

"We'll see," Kaylee grinned.

"Will you two stop arguing, you're making my headache worse," Hamon placed his hand on his forehead.

"Uh oh, you have a headache too," Amber asked. Hamon slumped his shoulders as he let his head limp. Lenard, Klyde and Kaylee all laughed at him.

Jean circled over to them, "Kaylee! He's about to try the meat!"

"Oh boy, I can't wait to see this," Lenard commented. Jean and Kaylee took off to watch.

The rest of the four approached the other side of the fire as well. Hamon took notice of Natalie, who was just beside them.

On the other side of the fire was Picc. Mark, another member of the group, sliced off a chunk of the monster. It was slimy in texture. It bounced and jiggled as Mark skinned the meat and placed it on a tray. The meat itself was pink, even after all the roasting it looked raw. Mark delivered it to Picc, who took the plate from his hands.

"Looks like it's happening," Hamon said. Picc grabbed a hold of the slab of meat. It molded and jiggled as Picc held it above his mouth. He lowered the meat into his mouth and took a sizable bite out of it. He cringed as the taste of the meat hit his tongue. There was no crunch and when swallowed, the entire bite traveled down his throat. Picc coughed into his hand as a tear swelled his eye.

"How was it?" Kaylee asked.

Picc cleared his throat, "Disgusting, but edible." He took large breaths in between words.

"You might have a better chance feeding me human feces than whatever the hell that was," Lenard stated.

"I'm right there with you," Mark made a disgusted face.

"I'm going to try some," Jean said as she approached Picc.

Hamon raised his hand and blocked her, "Let's wait to see what happens before anyone tries anything. We still don't know if there are any lasting effects from this…meat."

"I agree with Hamon, besides even if there aren't we still don't know if this stuff can harm you from eating too much," Alice mentioned.

"We won't find out unless we try it. If this is truly edible we won't have food problems for a while," Jean argued.

Alice raised her hands, "Then why don't we wait to see what happens to the new guy. I mean…isn't that the whole reason he said he would try it before anyone in the first place."

"Your sister's right," Lenard said.

"I just don't want us all to starve. Besides, Picc seems fine," she pointed.

"We don't have a damn clue what will happen to him, that's why we need to wait," Lenard said.

"Then what are we supposed to eat? How long are we supposed to wait? We only have enough MREs, the last the entire group a day or two at most. Just let Kaylee and I try some at least," she argued.

"Kaylee is not having any of that," Klyde said with his arms crossed and his chest puffed.

Kaylee's face morphed to disappointment, "Why not?"

"The same reason Lenard had. It's too uncertain." Klyde brought up a fair point. There was just too much unknown about this to jump to anything rash.

"I'm just going to try a bit with Jean, that's all," Kaylee said.

"Jean isn't trying anything," Alice stated.

"I don't need your permission to try it," Jean said.
Alice scoffed, "It doesn't matter if I do! I'm not letting you try any!"

"Alright, that's enough!" Hamon yelled. Everyone went silent as they gazed over to him. "We do not argue amongst ourselves! Right now, there's no rush to do anything, we have enough food to last us a couple of days. We'll give the new guy three days to see if anything happens, if not, then you could all have all the monster meat you could want. Right now, there's still something that needs to be answered."

He turned toward Picc, "You still haven't told us who you are, so get out with it."

Picc cleared his throat, "What is it you want to know about me?"

Hamon glared, "Don't play coy with me. You know exactly what we want to know. How did you know what that...pistol was."

"Oh well, to make a long story short, I have clear memories of the other world." Hamon squinted his eyes, he shifted his gaze to the rest of the camp, who also bared a confused expression.

"Be more specific," Hamon demanded.

"Well, it's hard to explain. You know how the *Appearers* have memories of another world, right?" The group nodded. "Well, I'm able to remember everything from the other world."

"Like the skies?" Amber questioned.

"Not just the skies. The civilizations, the farms, the people. The technology that they used. I remember all of it."

Hamon shook his head, "Civili...what are you talking about?" Each word he spoke sounded like an incantation. None of this he had ever heard before.

"Civilizations. A system of a population creating architecture, agriculture, cities...All of this we take a long time to explain. It's a system tasked with creating a survivable environment for a large group of people," Picc gestured his hands as he explained.

"How would they be able to do that with monsters all around?" Lenard interrogated. A good point. Massive societies with large groups of people seemed unlikely with monsters sprawled about.

Picc held up his finger, "That's the best part, there are no monsters. No darkness above them, the sun illuminates everything around them."

"What's the sun?" Hamon asked.

"A large bright sphere in the sky, so bright that even from millions of meters away it still casts a bright light on the plains," Picc said. It sounded crazy, but he swore that he had heard similar claims from *Appearers* before.

"Like anyone would believe that," Lenard scoffed.

"No, he's telling the truth. I remember it. I remember there being a bright circle in the sky," Amber said. That's right, Hamon had forgotten she had told stories about the sun before.

Lenard turned surprised. "I'm not lying, I'm telling the truth. When I appeared here six years ago I was left in contact with memories of everything. Those memories never disappeared," Picc insisted.

"Wait, so you know how people lived in that other world? Could you tell me about it?!" Kaylee begged.

"Hold on Kaylee, let us finish questioning him first," Hamon instructed. Kaylee slumped before she nodded and backed away.

"How can we trust you? How do we know you aren't making any of this up?" Hamon questioned.

"It's fine if you don't trust me, I wouldn't expect you to. But I do come with goodwill, I can use the knowledge I possess to help all of you. I wanted to do that with the group I previously was with. However, just like you, they didn't trust me."

"And what happened to them?" Hamon asked.

"I'm not sure. Some of them could have gotten away. Either way it's very unlikely that I'll ever see them again," he waved his hand toward the empty abyss.

Hamon glazed to the void, then cleared his throat and refocused on Picc, "The…memories that you possess, how can they help us?"

"I have knowledge of ways to gain an indefinite food supply. I also know of a way that we could push back and keep ourselves safe from the monsters. All you need to do is listen to me," Picc said.

Hamon raised an eyebrow, "What do you mean…push back the monsters?"

"We could fight them off. Truly, not just running away from them. As you can see, the flintlock pistol already demonstrated that," he pointed his hand toward the pistol that rested in his belt.

"You can't be serious, there's no way that pistol is enough to 'push back' the monsters," Lenard argued. Hamon found himself agreeing with Lenard.

Picc smiled as he bobbed his finger at him, "You're right, it's not. It takes too long to reload for the damage that it does. The only reason I was able to kill that monster was because I had a clear shot at it. If I had to improvise a shot, it most likely wouldn't be enough to kill. We need something else, something stronger…and I know exactly what that is."

"What?" Hamon asked.

"It's called a musket rifle. It operates similarly to the pistol, however, it's much stronger. Even without a clear shot it will kill any monster it's pointed at," Picc claimed.

"I've never heard or seen anything like that. And I've been venturing for twenty-five years," Klyde said.

"And therein lies the problem. The musket rifle is rare…very rare. Either it's the rarest item within the forest. Or it's so rare that anything rarer has never been found. The only reason I know it exists within the forest is because of two reasons.

One, *Appearers,* no matter how good their memory, will never remember an item that exists within the forest. Two, the one who told me about it was a *birthed one.* Specifically a very old person who claimed that saw it once as a child and witnessed its power. What convinces me he wasn't lying is that I do have memories of weapons similar to the musket from the other world. But I have no memories of the musket itself."

"That doesn't prove anything," Lenard argued.

"I'm well aware. However, if the musket is really as powerful as described, I believe the risk to find it is worth it," Picc said.

"Hold on…none of us are going anywhere to find anything. We aren't chasing after a legend," Hamon stated.

"Wait…we should think about this. I mean, if this weapon really is real, then we wouldn't have to worry about monsters ever again," Jarold said.

"I'm on Jarold's side. It's at least worth it to do some looking," Quinton placed his hand on Jarold's shoulder.

"Are you guys seriously letting this guy fool you, he's a nut. There's no such thing as a musket rifle," Lenard mocked.

"Perhaps you all should discuss this amongst yourselves before you come to a conclusion. It doesn't appear you all are on the same page," Picc said.

"Don't act like you know us," Lenard glared daggers.

"No…he's right…all of you wait over by the second fire. I'll join all of you in a second," Hamon said. If they were going to come to a decision like this, then the entire group should have a say in it.

Lenard nodded. The group followed each other to the second fire and out of hearing distance. Hamon approached Picc.

"Is there something you have to tell me?" Picc asked.

He knelt down to face him, and stared into his soul, "I don't know who you are…but if you cause trouble for this group…I will kill you."

"Understood…but I assure you I only want to help. But if I were you…I would worry more about how they may feel," Picc said. Hamon's gaze softened.

It was a good point. His group was more than anxious to get back out there. He was certain that the sound of them finding something that could make their lives much better would get any of them excited, even if it might just be a fantasy, barring Klyde and Lenard. He turned his back to Picc to join the other venturers.

Chapter 3

Decisions To Be Made

The group huddled around the fire. They positioned themselves in a circle around the flame.

Hamon stepped forward, "It seems that not all of us seem to see eye to eye. However, from what I can see, no one wants to speak up first." Despite heated arguments not too early ago, the group stood awkward. "I guess I'll start then. I see absolutely no reason why we should even think about venturing into the woods for a…fantasy. We have no idea if this thing even exists."

"Even if the musket doesn't exist…is there not a chance we could at least find more pistols?" Jarold proposed.

"It's not worth the risk. We've survived just fine with hatches and spears," Hamon argued.

Quinton sneered, "Survived just fine? Why are you acting like nothing is going on? Are expeditions are growing longer. It's getting harder and harder to find a decent amount of food. And the longer we're out in the woods, the more likely a monster attack is to happen."

"I know…but chasing after a mystery weapon won't help anything. We'll only lead ourselves into more danger," Hamon said.

"And how long before our expeditions for food turns from hours to days? From days to weeks? We can't afford that. Especially when those expeditions can lead to finding other venturers that we'll have to take care of," Quinton said.

"I'm with Quinton on this. I know some of us aren't as fond of *The Forest* as the others, but you have to admit we can't just keep doing the same thing. Something needs to change," Jarold stated.

"What's the point of changing things if it's just going to get us all killed?" Lenard argued. He made a good point, as much as Hamon knew he only said it out of cynicism.

"Maybe it will get us all killed. But what's the point of not taking a risk if resources are going to deplenish, Quinton said. He was right about one thing, something did have to change. Hamon just saw no reason as to why that change should be chasing after something that might not even be real.

"Quinton's right. It's a risk with high reward versus no risk with no reward. If we take this chance and it pays off we could be in the best position we've ever been in," Jean stated.

"That's if it even pays off. You guys aren't considering that even if we do find this…musket, it might not even do anything," Alice mentioned.

"It's still worth the risk!" Jean yelled.

"Alright! That's enough…we'll put it to a vote," Hamon suggested.

"I guess we could do that…but that's not exactly fair. Most people are going to vote to not go," Kaylee stated.

"It's as fair as could possibly be. Obviously arguing isn't going to take us anywhere, so we'll handle it based on the majority. Either you vote for the expedition, you vote against it or you don't vote at all. Let's start with those who are against the expedition, raise your hands."

Hamon, Lenard, Alice and Amber raised their hands.

"Alright, so that's four in favor of not going, who is in favor of going?"

Kaylee, Jean, Quinton and Jarold raised their hands.

"Looks like it's a tie…" As soon as Hamon spoke, Klyde raised his hand. Hamon turned his head toward him with an expanded expression. Even Amber and Kaylee looked shocked.

"I vote in favor of going," Klyde stated. This was very unlike him. He's a very logical and practical person. Him of all people should understand how ridiculous chasing after a myth is.

"What!? Why!?" Lenard interrogated.

"...I've gone on many expeditions. Survived with countless groups. It all ended the same way. They were always too stubborn. I don't like the idea of it, but I think this goes beyond what I think. This isn't just about us. I may live long enough to be fed…to have my needs met. But if our supplies are really going to keep dwindling…I think it's important to leave the next generation with something to hope for. I think it's time for us to stop being stubborn and try something else. With all due respect Hamon, your way isn't going to work forever," Klyde glared.

"What kind of *bullshit* is that?" Lenard questioned. Hamon himself tried to find points to argue against Klyde, but he could not think of anything.

"Lenard…that's enough, I think Klyde has a point. Does anyone else have anything to say against that?" Hamon asked the group, who remained silent. "Then it's settled…the expedition is happening…we'll take some time to prepare, let's say two weeks. Then we'll head out."

Kaylee and Jean smiled with glee. Lenard scoffed as he fled from the circle into one of the tents.

Klyde approached Hamon's side, "You think he's going to be okay?"

"Lenard will be fine," Hamon said. He's handled far worse than people disagreeing with him, although it was one of his weaknesses.

"I don't know…he's been acting a bit harsher since you guys got back," Klyde eye'd him.

"He's gone through worse. For right now…why don't we discuss who we're going to bring. I think it should be a group of four, that sized group tends to be more successful on expeditions," Hamon said.

"Should I come?" Klyde asked.

"No…if this expedition is going to happen I want to be there. And at least one of us needs to be at the camp in case of a monster attack. Just stay here, spend some time with Amber and Kaylee," Hamon instructed.

"I won't argue with that…but I think Picc might have some ideas in mind, you should ask him," Klyde pointed toward Picc, who sat at the center fire.

"...Alright…" Hamon whispered. Another talk with Picc did not sound too enticing. He had only known him for a couple hours, yet he managed to become a massive pain in the ass.

Klyde rested his hand on Hamon's shoulder, "But first…why don't you get some rest. You still haven't had the chance to sit down and relax since the expedition."

"You're probably right…I shouldn't be making big decisions tired huh," Hamon shrugged.

"I'll watch over the camp while you rest. We'll talk about preparations once you're done resting," Klyde offered.

Hamon nodded as he too entered into one of the tents. Klyde turned back toward the camp. Hamon glanced toward the camp. The members were all spread out and kept to themselves. He could see Klyde's shadowed outline standing outside the camp. Klyde's silhouette traveled to the center fire.

"We came to a vote…the expedition is happening." Klyde's voice came through muffled by the tents fabric.

"That's great news. I have some ideas as to who can come along," Picc said.

"We'll discuss that at a later point once Hamon is done resting. In the meantime, I have some questions I want to ask you." Hamon shrugged as he laid down and shut his eyes.

Hamon exited the tent. He rubbed the gunk from his eyes, then gazed upon the site. The rest of the group seemed to all fall asleep themselves as he was the only one who seemed to be outside. Except for Klyde, who stood near the campfire where Picc also sat. He approached them.

Klyde turned to see Hamon. "What happened while I was out?" Hamon asked.

"I asked Picc some questions. Just some basic things about his experience with venturing and all that. Aswell as a few questions about this other world," he answered.

He furrowed his brow, "Find anything out?"

"Well, he's decent at venturing. He claims he's had a few run-ins with monsters and even claimed to outrun one. He certainly won't be a hindrance once we take him on this expedition," Klyde said.

"What about the other world?" He questioned.

"Everything he's told me about it matches up with things Amber's told me about her memories. There's no reason to doubt anything he's saying," Klyde assured.

Then it's likely he's not faking it then, Hamon thought. He stretched his arm, "I guess that's good to hear. So then…we should discuss who's going on this venture."

"I think it should be four people not including Picc," Klyde suggested.

"That many people? That could pose a hazard, don't you think?" He asked while kneeling down and stretching his leg. Five people was quite the crowd, especially when their average expedition only included three.

"This expedition is going to be long. You're going to need as many people as you can get to carry as much supplies as possible. Four people is the most we can do without posing a risk to the camp itself. Besides, if you're bringing that pistol, running into a monster shouldn't be as dangerous. Just keep a close eye out."

"Alright…if you say so. Right now we know for sure it's going to be Picc and I. I was thinking of bringing along Lenard," Hamon said.

Klyde furrowed his brow, “Are you sure that’s a good idea? No offense to Lenard but he’s not exactly an expert. I would think you’d want to bring along someone else.”

“Lenard is smart. He knows when we're in over our heads and it's time for us to bail out. If this were a normal expedition I would think about bringing Jarold instead. But he can get kind of arrogant. I want to bring along Quinton and Mark as well,” Hamon said.

“Not a bad choice. I’m assuming you’re bringing those two for their strength?” Klyde asked.

“That’s right. You said it yourself, we need to get as much supplies as possible and there’s nobody better at luggaging than those two.” They were the most physically fit of the entire camp. At most, they could reasonably carry around fifty pounds on their back.

“If you would allow me to…I have a suggestion as well,” Picc raised his hand.

Hamon glanced down toward him, “What would that be?”

“The young girl…I don’t remember her name. The one with blue eyes, we need to bring her,” he stated.

Hamon raised an eyebrow, “You mean Kaylee?” He questioned.

“Yes, her. Those blue eyes of hers will be extremely helpful,” Picc smiled.

Her blue eyes? Hamon questioned in his own head. “No…no! We’re not bringing her,” Hamon declared.

“Why not?” Picc raised his eyebrow.

“Because she’s a child. She’s not ready to go on an expedition…especially not one like this.” He had little hope she could make it out there, especially in a long expedition like this one.

"An expedition like this is exactly why we should bring her," Picc gestured his hands.

"Wait…you said something about her blue eyes? What is that about?" Klyde questioned.

"Blue eyes reflect more light than brown or black eyes do. From what I can tell, her and the older woman, who I assume is her mother, are the only ones that possess eyes like that."

"How does…reflecting more light help us?" Hamon interrogated.

"It means she can see in the dark better. And not just a little better…a lot better. Back in my old group, one of the members had blue eyes. They were able to see monsters coming almost minutes ahead of everyone else. An ability like that for an expedition like this is irreplaceable. We would be idiotic to not bring her along," Picc explained.

An ability to see better in the dark, then it did sound priceless. However, "Bringing her is out of the question. She's a kid, still too immature for this kind of thing. We have plenty of members who are able to get us out of trouble quickly. There's no sense in bringing a child," Hamon argued.

Picc raised an eyebrow, "And how exactly is she supposed to learn cooped up in the campsite all her life. Bringing her with you can give her plenty of experience out in *The Forest*."

"She can also be killed, and that's not a risk I'm willing to take," Hamon stated.

"There will be pretty much no risk at all…as long as I have the pistol, lining up a shot to kill won't be too difficult," Picc claimed.

Hamon clenched his fist, "I don't give a damn if the odds are a million to one. If there is any risk at all of Kaylee being hurt or killed then she's not coming."

"I know it sounds risky," Picc raised his palms, "but think about how much she could help. She would be able to point out camps before we could. See monsters before we could. We can't waste an opportunity like that."

"Shut it!" Klyde yelled at him. He approached Picc and stood right above him once more then slapped Picc clean across the face.

"My daughter is not some…opportunity! She's not coming and that's final. If you even so much as imply bringing her again I will cast you out of here myself…understood!" He stated.

"Fools…" Picc bitterly whispered. Klyde rolled his eyes and walked away.

"Ignore him, we'll go with the group I proposed," Hamon stated.

"I would get them ready now, tell them what you want them to do and their role. I'm going to go get some rest. I'm starting to feel like I could use some," Klyde sighed.

"No problem, rest up." Klyde turned his back toward him and headed for one of the tents. Hamon went his own way. He stopped by each tent that Quinton and Mark were resting at. He led them over to the main campfire with Picc. Once they were lined up he turned back toward Lenard's tent.

Hamon knelt down just outside the tent, "Lenard! We need you out here!" Rustling could be heard. Lenard exited the tent.

"Did you have to wake me up? I would prefer to sleep," Lenard complained.

"I'm aware. We need you out at the main campfire. Quinton and Mark are already over there."

Lenard nodded as he followed Hamon. Once they arrived at the campfire Hamon positioned the three of them in a line. Hamon took position in front of the group.

"Let's get this out right now…You three are the ones I have decided to join Picc and I on the expedition. Do you have any questions about that?" Hamon asked.

"Why are we bringing so many people? Couldn't that leave the campsite in danger?" Mark questioned.

"Klyde will be here to watch over the camp. He is more than capable of keeping the camp safe on his own. We need to bring a lot of people because this expedition will yield plenty of supplies. Even if we don't find the musket, we still need to hold on to all the supplies we can get. Which means all of us will be bringing backpacks. And all of us should be prepared to carry those back when full. Any more questions?" Hamon asked.

"How long are we going on this expedition for?" Quinton asked.

Hamon gestured toward the bags they scattered the ground near the fire, "Until all of our backpacks are entirely full or we run into a monster. Most likely the ladder so all of you need to be on guard. Because we'll most likely get attacked by a monster, we'll be bringing the torches instead of the lantern."

"If we're going to be going on such a long expedition, how are we going to mark the way back? It's not like we have enough stone to mark a path that long," Lenard mentioned.

"I have something we could use for that," Picc said.

"What is that?" Lenard raised an eyebrow.

“I have a compass. It’s a device that will help us tell which direction we’re going,” Picc explained.

“Let me see it,” Hamon requested.

Picc reached into one of his back pockets and pulled out a circle of iron. He handed it to Hamon who analyzed it. He noticed the needle on the top.

“What is this needle?” Hamon questioned. It moved slightly in various different directions. Four letters were placed on each end of the circle.

“It always points in the same direction. If you want to find your way back here, all you need is to know the direction of the camp relative to the direction of the needle,” Picc said.

“That seems a little too reliable. Is there some sort of catch?” Lenard asked.

“None,” Picc shrugged. “It’s not like the needle is just going to suddenly stop working.”

“How does this thing work anyway?” Hamon wondered. He noticed the letters on it were the same as some of the ancient maps they would stumble upon every once in a while.

“It uses a magnetic force to point in the direction of greatest magnetic magnitude,” he rambled.

Lenard arched an eyebrow, “What the hell does that mean?”

“It means it will always point in the same direction. That’s all you need to know.”

“Fine, so long as it serves as a good way to get back,” Hamon said.

“Was there anything else you wanted to mention about the expedition?” Quinton steered the conversation back on track.

"Um…yes. For food, we'll all have two MREs for each of us. I know that's not a lot but we're still low on food, so it's the best we can do. We'll all also have two flasks of water, bandages and extra clothing. I'll be bringing my hatchet, Picc can bring the pistol. If there are any weapons you would like to carry you are welcome to.

"However, that will come at the cost of weight, so don't get overly paranoid. The trek starts two weeks from now. In the meantime I will take responsibility for training some of you up. Mainly you Mark, since you are still inexperienced."

"That's fine with me," Mark nodded.

"Alright. All of you get ready, understand." All of them nodded. "Then you can all go back to resting."

Quinton and Mark went back to their tents. Lenard remained behind. He wore an uneasy gaze. "What is it Learned?" Hamon asked.

"I…are we really doing this? I still don't think this is a great idea. I mean, we'll be leaving the camp to fend for itself pretty much."

"Even if we don't find anything, we'll still need the supplies. We should probably start going on longer expeditions like this anyway. Are there any other concerns that you have?"

"I don't feel good about leaving the camp behind…I know it's a bit irrational, but it just doesn't sit right with me."

"You don't have to worry. You know Klyde will handle the camp fine on his own."

"I'm aware…It's just an irrational concern," Lenard said.

"If you want, you can stay here. We'll find someone else to come with us," Hamon offered.

Lenard's eyes widened. "No…no, I'll come. There's got to be someone there to watch over you guys."

"That's exactly why I want to have you along. Now go get some rest, seriously. You'll need it," Hamon shot him a smile.

"Fine," Lenard sighed as he walked away. Hamon watched as Lenard entered the tent. He stood there in a quiet moment. With only the crackling of the fire.

"You're going to regret not taking the girl along. Those eyes of hers are truly an invaluable asset. Maybe even more so than the musket rifle," Picc interrupted.

"You shut your mouth. Otherwise I'll get Klyde back over here to deal with you," Hamon warned.

"Who knows…maybe she will come along. I mean, she seemed to love asking me questions about *The Forest*. She must have a deep curiosity about it. She might even demand to come along when she finds out," Picc said.

"I don't care if she knows or not. She's not coming along," Hamon declared.

"You can say that all you want. But the girl's nearly eighteen. She might not think there is a need to listen to you," he spoke with a smug smile.

Hamon's glare softened. He was well aware of Kaylee's growing spirit. It wouldn't be too long before she would be joining them. Whether Hamon liked it or not. "She's not coming with us…and that's final, you understand."

"Fine, but I still want to be there when she does go on her first expedition. I really want to see those eyes in action once more," he whispered.

Hamon scoffed and then turned his back toward Picc, then walked toward a tent. He opened the zipper and stepped onto the polyester floor. He laid on his back and placed his hands behind his head. He worried about Kaylee. He had no doubt in his mind that what Picc said about her eyes are true.

She always seemed to see things before everyone else. She never had any problem with seeing out further into the forest than the others. He wondered if that was what made Kaylee have such an adventurous spirit in the first place. She did seem to stare out into the distance more than the others. She was like himself in that way.

He clenched his eyes closed and turned his head so his cheek was planted on the ground. The rough ground smashed his face. He sighed as his thoughts began to fade.

Chapter 4

Preparations

Hamon patted Mark on the back after they finished another training session. At this stage, Mark had learned the proper way to dodge a monster while he carried luggage, as well as how to wield a spear that he had wished to bring. Mark rejoined with the rest of the group, while Hamon returned to Quinton.

The expedition had grown within the minds of the group. Hamon could tell because of how much he could hear the members whisper about it to each other. It was even titled by them as the Grand Expedition. He had further discussed how the expedition would go with Picc and Lenard. They would leave once everyone was rested and prepared, then venture out for at least five days. They decided if no musket were found at that time they would return to camp using the compass. Picc had taught the other members how to use it.

Hamon discussed with Quinton about how items would be stored. He had plotted that Lenard and him would carry lighter items like clothing or small tools, while Quinton and Mark would carry food, water and heavier tools.

Some commotion went on as they talked. A large conversation between many members echoed from a distance. Then, Mark approached them.

"Hey, Hamon. We've got a problem," Mark warned.

"What is it?" Hamon asked.

"The food supply, we've only got a dozen or so MREs left," he said.

Hamon's eyebrow arched, "What? We had over fifty just two weeks ago? What happened?"

"We only had thirty MREs two weeks ago," Quinton corrected. He had forgotten how low they had been on food with all the planning that had been going on.

"Shit…that changes things. Mark is going to have to stay here," Hamon sighed. Mark was the only one capable of keeping the group fed off of different plants found in the wild.

Quinton raised his fingers to his chin, "That certainly does change things. Are you sure we can't just leave Klyde to handle it? I know he's not as good of a cook but he can certainly make things edible."

Hamon shook his head, "No…Klyde has enough he needs to deal with. He can't keep watch over the camp while cooking food for everyone at the same time. It's fine, we'll continue with the same strategy without Mark. We'll all just have to carry more than we expected."

"Or we can find someone else from the camp to go on the expedition. I'm sure Jarold would suffice," Quinton shrugged.

"I already explained why I don't want to bring him. It's not like anyone else is able to. Amber wouldn't make it, Alice would be too concerned over Jean, whether we bring her or her sister and Klyde is too busy watching over the camp. We don't have anyone to spare," Hamon said.

Quinton's gaze lightened, "What about Kaylee?"

Hamon glared, "No. I told you multiple times why I can't allow that."

"Alright, alright," Quinton waved his hands in a defensive manner. "I guess we could just move things around. Are you sure you can't bring Jarold? You seem to not get along with him very well."

Hamon exhaled, "Jarold is young. He thinks because he is an *Appearer* that somehow makes him special. Like he has some grand purpose here. That's good for small expeditions as it keeps the group morale up. But for something like this it isn't going to be anything but a hindrance. All three of us factoring for Mark will be more than enough."

"You say all that about Jarold but you always defend Lenard. Why is that?" Quinton questioned.

"I know a lot of you don't get along with him, but he is a good venturer. I know, I've gone on expeditions with him more than anyone else," Hamon claimed.

A look of disdain formed on Quinton's face, "Are you sure you're not just playing favorites with Lenard because he's the only venturer from your old group?"

"I've considered that multiple times. I really do think Lenard is just better for this situation. Is there a reason why you think I'm playing favorites?" Hamon glared in response.

"I think you're trying to assemble a team that will be easiest for you to deal with. I can tell you want to go on this expedition for just the supplies. But others here genuinely do want to find that musket, including me," He pointed his index finger at his chest. "Don't make everything go your way because you think you know what's best."

"I'll keep that in mind…" Quinton nodded as he walked away. Maybe he was being biased about this whole thing. As much as he didn't believe it, there were a few members of the group that were hoping to find the musket. Hamon wasn't as cynical about the forest as Lenard was, but he did agree with him a lot.

Klyde had him beat in terms of overall experience, but Hamon was the youngest when he started venturing than anyone else in the group. Like Lenard, he had little belief that *The Forest* had anything good to offer. But maybe this was different. Maybe he should feel different about this. He pondered as he continued his work. Kaylee wondered to him not much later.

"Hey Hamon," Kaylee greeted.

"Hey…why are you not waiting with the rest?" Hamon questioned.

"Well, I just felt like wandering around," she shrugged as she pursed her lips. "I wanted to talk to you about this big expedition. Feels like we never really got to talk about it."

Hamon squinted, "What's there to discuss? It's the same thing we always do, just longer."

A smirk formed on Kaylee's face, "That's not true, you're chasing after a super cool legend about a powerful weapon. How could that not be super cool."

"Oh yeah…right. What is it you want to talk about?" Hamon asked.

Kaylee's mouth gaped as she gestured her arms out wide, "About the musket…do you really think it's out there?"

Hamon shrugged, “I don’t know…I’ve never seen it. But that doesn’t mean it’s not real. Maybe it is out there.” He wondered why she was questioning this now.

“I never got to hear any of your stories of venturing. It’s crazy to me that I haven’t,” Kaylee laughed. Her statement rung true. He had plenty of stories to share with her.

His gaze fell, “I don’t really like talking about those times.”

“You’ve had bad experiences, right?” Kaylee asked.

“Yes…many. That’s why I’m so reluctant to bring you. A good kid like yourself shouldn’t be out there. You should be here, where it’s safe,” Hamon said.

Kaylee sighed as her shoulders slumped, “I know…but I can’t help it. I really want to know what’s out there. Even if it ends up like nothing that I hoped for, nothing ventured, nothing gained, right?”

Hamon sighed. If he kept Kaylee away…would that be one of the biases Quinton had called him out on. He knew that Quinton had been training her. He would see them spar often. She worked hard to come along and it might have been his own weakness that kept her away.

“...if joining us is something you’re serious about…I suggest talking to your father about it,” Hamon whispered. Kaylee’s eyes widened. Slowly a smile plastered across her face. She leaped into Hamon as she embraced him with her arms.

“Thank you,” she muttered. Hamon smiled as he hugged her as well. They shared a brief moment of affirmation before Kaylee backed away. He thought to himself that perhaps this was the right call.

"Like I said though. It's a matter of what your father has to say. It's not up to me," Hamon explained.

"Understood," Kaylee nodded. She joyfully stepped off into the distance. Hamon was left with a mix of different emotions swirling through him. That sense of uncertainty plagued his consciousness. He wanted to have hope that Kaylee would do well for herself, but hope was something that was often squandered from him.

Kaylee, now with newfound confidence, made her way over to her father and mother. They rested at the fire at the edge of the campsite. The two of them seemed to be only enjoying each other's company.

Klyde was the first to notice Kaylee's approach. "What is it you want?" He asked right as Kaylee stopped in front of them. They were cuddled next to each other by the bonfire, Amber had her head rested on his shoulder.

"I have something crazy to ask you…could I join Hamon and the others on the grand expedition?" Kaylee politely begged.

"No," Klyde and Amber said in unison. Kaylee slumped her shoulders. She had anticipated that response. However, she had to continue this argument somehow.

"Please, I just want an opportunity to prove myself." She pleaded by clasping her hands together.

"You can prove yourself on some other expedition. Why does it need to be this one?" Amber asked. She lifted her head from Klyde's shoulder to focus her glance at her. She made a valid point, Kaylee could just venture on any other expedition. However, those expeditions did not include finding the musket. It was that little detail that made her want to join no matter the consequences.

"Because they could use the help. I could take the part that Mark was supposed to handle," Kaylee said.

"No…you can stay here and help me look over the camp. But you are not going on that expedition," Klyde stood upright and towered over Kaylee. His broad shoulders covered her view of her mother.

Kaylee crossed her arms, "Why not?" She knew she was being a bit immature. She felt it in her bones but ignored it regardless.

"They're going to be in the forest for days. That's too much for someone like you. I can't let you go," he leaned over and wrapped her arm around her shoulder.

"Dad…two weeks ago you said to yourself that this wasn't about you. You said it was about us," Kaylee gestured her hands toward herself.

"I was talking about opportunities, not this. And from what I remember you were fine with not going yourself," Klyde noted.

Kaylee clenched her fists, "Well…something changed."

"Did Picc rope you into this?" Klyde sneered.

"Huh?…no…Hamon said something to me. Why would Picc want me to come?" Kaylee questioned. She could not think of a single reason as to why Picc would want her to join. Klyde's eyes widened as he realized what he had just said. There was something that he knew that she did not.

"Are you hiding something from me?" Kaylee questioned.

Amber looked toward him out of curiosity herself. "It was nothing. Don't worry about it," he excused. It tufted her somewhat that her father would not just tell her.

Kaylee glared at him, "Don't lie to me. Just tell me what he said," she stated.

Klyde sighed, "He said something about your eyes…something about them being able to see in the dark better…I don't know."

Kaylee arched an eyebrow, "How am I able to see in the dark better?" As she processed the thought, she realized what it could be referring to. She did have memories of seeing better than other members.

"He said it was because of the color of your eyes. You have blue eyes, apparently they see in the dark better than brown eyes. I forgot the reason why," he squinted his brow.

Kaylee unwrapped herself from her father's grasp and stared at him, "You were going to keep that secret from me?" It was more of a question out of dumbfoundness. She would have to find out about that eventually, so she wondered why it was kept secret in the first place.

"Yes…because I didn't want you to go. And I knew if you found out about that there would be no stopping you from going," Klyde said.

"So he wants me on the team because I can see really well. Okay…regardless of that I still want to go," she stated.

"You know exactly why I can't let you do that," he pointed at her.

Amber circled around him and faced Kaylee herself, "Your father's right, it's too dangerous for you," she added.

"I know…" Kaylee sighed. In all reality, there was a good chance she could lose her life on this expedition. She needed to do something, however. She wanted to do anything other than nothing.

"Then why do you need to go on this one?" Amber questioned.

"Because…I want to find that musket," she gestured to the gap in the trees to the abyss. "If it really is out there then I want to help find it. If we do…then maybe we can go to that other world you and Picc always talk about."

Amber's shoulders limped, "Kaylee…"

Kaylee stepped in front of her before she could speak, "I know you don't put much stock into it but I do. And now that Picc is here there's more proof that we can get to the other world."

"That's not a good reason for you to go on this expedition," Klyde said.

She raised her fists, "It's an opportunity. It's an opportunity to find something that can change our lives. I want to be a part of that. I want to help. And if I can do that by going on this expedition then that's what I am going to do."

"…You said that Hamon was the one who said you could come, correct?" Klyde asked.

She nodded, "Yeah. He said it was up to you though."

"Bring him here so I can talk to him," Klyde instructed. Kaylee bit her lip, and glazed back and forth in a nervous manner, "You're not going to get mad at him, are you?" She asked.

"Just go get him." Kaylee nodded as she turned away. Klyde sat back down and gazed into the fire.

Kaylee arrived dragging Hamon by his arm a short while later. He wore an anxious gaze and bit his lip. Klyde stood upright and faced Hamon, who met his gaze.

"Here he is," Kaylee gestured her arms toward Hamon with a nervous smile on her face. She took a couple steps back to let the two of them talk.

"Thank you," Klyde expressed. "Now, if you two could, would you mind letting us talk alone for a bit," he gestured toward another side of the camp.

Kaylee and Amber nodded. Amber stood up from the ground and wrapped her arm around Kaylee's waist. The two walked out of visibility.

"Are you mad at me about this?" Hamon asked with a worried expression of someone who thought they were about to get punched in the face.

Klyde exhaled as his hands pressed against his hips, "I don't know…I feel like I should be. You went against the whole idea of this expedition and that she could come. Why change your mind?"

"Because of something Quinton told me. Kaylee wants to find that musket more than anyone here. As much as I hate to admit it, she would be the perfect fit for this team. Without her it wouldn't be fair to the people that genuinely want to find that musket. It wouldn't be fair toward you," Hamon said.

Klyde crossed his arms, "You think having her on the team is going to make you more likely to find that musket?"

Hamon shook his head, "No…Kaylee's eyes will help us do that. Her spirit will keep us looking for it in the first place."

"Hmm…Kaylee, come back over here!" Klyde yelled over to her. Kaylee turned her head toward him. Klyde waved his hand, then she nodded as she approached them.

"What is it?" Kaylee asked.

Klyde placed his hands on Kaylee's shoulders, "If you are going on this expedition…I want you to promise me one thing. Listen to Hamon, don't you even think about disobeying him. Listen to Quinton and Lenard as well, they know *The Forest* far better than you do, don't act like they don't. You understand me?"

"Wait…you're letting me go?" Kaylee asked.

"...I…I would still prefer it if you didn't. However, if I were to force you to stay here…that wouldn't be fair to you. So…if you truly want to…go out there…and bring home that musket," Klyde smiled.

Kaylee smiled back. She knelt into him and she wrapped her arms around him. Klyde hugged her back. He squeezed her tight. His arms tensed with fear of the unknown.

"Be careful, okay," Klyde requested as he let her go.

"I know…I'll try," She nodded.

"Hamon?" Klyde turned toward him. Hamon snapped his attention to Klyde.

He placed his hand on his shoulder as well as Kaylee's. "Keep her safe. Don't let her get out of line. You know how she can get."

"I'll protect her with my life," Hamon raised his fist to his chest.

Klyde once again turned back toward Kaylee, "Kaylee…I know you want to prove yourself. But don't act too courageously. Keep your eyes open. Don't let anything sneak up on you."

"Understood," she nodded.

"Well then," Hamon wrapped his arm around Kaylee's shoulder. "I think you and I should get you prepped now."

"Okay! Oh…wait, we still have to talk to mom about this, don't we?" Kaylee realized.

"Don't worry about her…I'll handle talking to her. You two go ahead and get ready," Klyde waved her off.

Hamon and Kaylee nodded. Hamon led Kaylee toward the central campfire. Klyde went off to talk to Amber. At the central campfire was Picc. he was still sitting down at the tree next to the campfire. He seemed to draw an attraction to sitting there.

Hamon stepped over to him, "Picc…looks like you win. Kaylee is joining us."

Picc immediately smiled with delight. "That's good news! Finally I get to see those eyes in action again!"

Hamon raised his palm, "Calm down-"

Kayle jumped in between them, "So! I heard you were saying there was something special about my eyes!" Kaylee interrupted. Hamon scoffed.

"Yes! You're blue eyes!" Picc pointed at her eyes.

"How does that work? Why does my eyes being blue make them see better?" Kaylee questioned.

"Everything we see is light waves. You see light is a wave of different visible colors that bounce or absorb into objects. Certain colors bounce or absorb this light better. This allows you to see better in the dark than people with darker colored eyes like brown or amber," Kaylee nodded along. Her curiosity grew with each word Picc spoke.

"You said you knew someone else who had blue eyes?" Hamon asked.

"That's correct," he raised his index finger. "Someone from my previous group. Although their eyes were more hazel then they were blue. Kaylee has true blue eyes. Which means her eyes should work even better than the other one."

"Is the only added bonus seeing in the dark better?" Hamon raised an eyebrow. With the way Picc had talked about it, he assumed it might mean Kaylee has special powers or something.

Picc scoffed as he waved his hand at Hamon, "You make it seem like that's nothing special. Even the previous person I knew could see monsters far before anyone else. Kaylee should be able to do even more than that."

"I just want to know in case there are any other abilities that could be useful to us," Hamon stated.

Picc smiled, "Trust me, that one ability will be more than helpful enough."

Kaylee waved her arm up and down, "Hey, if I have true blue eyes does that mean I have the best set of eyes?" she asked.

"I heard legends of venturers who possessed white eyes. I've never seen a venturer like that myself. And I have no true way to prove it," Picc shrugged.

"We're getting sidetracked here…Kaylee let me give you a rundown of the plan," Hamon grabbed her shoulder. "We're all going to have two MREs and two flasks of water. Do you have any knowledge of weaponry?"

She nodded, "Yeah, Quinton gave me a good run down on everything I need to know." Of course Quinton would prepare ahead like that.

"What weapons did he teach you to use?" Hamon asked.

"Just the spear. That's the only thing he had time to train me with," she shrugged.

"Then you'll bring that. But keep in mind how much that weighs. If you get tired from lifting something we aren't going to be able to carry it for you," Hamon said.

Kaylee waved her hands at him, "I understand. Quinton's already given me the ground rules of expeditions plenty of times."

"I'm aware. I'm sure he's told you about the no-talking rule, correct?" Hamon asked.

"Yes," she nodded.

"You can disregard that rule for this expedition," he said.

She raised an eyebrow, "How come?"

"We'll be bringing the torch instead of the lantern. We won't have to worry as much about monsters, but try not to talk too much, alright," Hamon said.

"You got it, sir," she gave an exaggerated salute. "Is there anything else I need to know?" She asked.

"One last thing…If you do run into a monster, don't go running off on your own. Follow the torch bearer, in this case I'm the torch bearer. Wherever you see me running, you follow. Unless I tell you otherwise, understand?" Hamon asked.

"Understood," she nodded.

"We'll leave her early tomorrow…18 hours from now. You've got any issue with that?" Hamon questioned.

"Nope," Kaylee shook her head.

"Then go get some rest," Hamon instructed as he tapped her shoulder and pointed to one of the tents. She let out a sigh, then nodded as walked toward the tent. She opened the zipper and entered it.

"18 hours from now…when is that?" Picc questioned.

"Should be somewhere around three o'clock," Hamon answered.

"AM or PM?" Hamon raised an eyebrow. "Oh right…you wouldn't know that. Makes sense, since you only have mechanical clocks here. I was talking about something from the other world. You are aware that a full day is twenty-four hours, correct?" Picc asked.

"Of course I do. We have a calendar as well, you know," Hamon said. Before Hamon and Picc could continue their conversation Lenard came rushing toward them.

A worried expression plastered his face and he looked sweaty and concerned. "Hamon, what the hell is going on?" he asked.

"What is it?" Hamon questioned.

"Kaylee…Amber just told me that Klyde is letting her come with," his fists clenched.

"Oh…yeah…Klyde and I both had a discussion about it and we came to the conclusion that she would come," Hamon stood firm.

"Why? She's just a kid…she shouldn't be going on an expedition like this," he gestured toward the tent she had entered.

Hamon raised his palm at him, "I get your concerns but like I said, we've discussed it already. Kaylee joining the team is the best course of action."

Lenard sneered, "Why?"

"Because without her we won't stay on track for the whole reason we agreed on this expedition in the first place," Hamon crossed his arms.

Lenard raised his forearms as he glared at Hamon, "The whole reason we went on this expedition in the first place is bullshit. And I remember not agreeing to this to begin with."

"Lenard…I understand your concerns. And I agree with you, I don't think the musket is any more real than you think it is," Hamon placed his hand on his chest. "That's exactly why I'm bringing her. If you're really that concerned about it then help me keep her safe out there."

Lenard sighed, "...fine…but if anything happens to her I'm putting that on you."

A smile formed on Hamon's face, "I would be disappointed in you if you didn't." He turned his back toward Hamon and walked away.

"He doesn't seem to be too happy about this," Picc said.

"No shit," Hamon scoffed. He still had little faith that Picc would make for a good venturing partner, but Lenard was right about one thing. During the couple weeks he has been here, he seemed to have no fear whatsoever.

"That's someone you want on this team. He seems a tad immature," Picc insulted.

"Yet he's more compassionate than you could ever hope to be," Hamon countered.

Picc snickered, "Compassion won't get us anywhere."

"But it will keep us human, and that's far more important," Hamon laid an intimidating gaze.

Picc rolled his eyes in a cocky manner. Hamon shook his head as he stepped away from him. He still found it hard to believe that they were going to do this. He never thought this would happen. Yet...now he felt like he should hold out a little hope that they might just find something out there.

Chapter 5

The Grand Expedition

The venturers awaited at the edge of the camp. Hamon watched as the venturers gave their goodbyes. Some teared up, others were happy. The atmosphere of the whole thing made Hamon's sense of uncertainty grow.

Klyde and Amber hounded Kaylee and gave her lecture after lecture about the do's and don'ts of *The Forest*. Kaylee had heard all these lectures a million times from Quinton already. Despite that she did her best to not appear bothered by the advice as she understood her parents' concern.

After Amber finished her fifteenth lecture, she turned to Hamon and approached him. "Be safe out there," she wished him.

"I'll try my best," Hamon tapped his hand on Amber's shoulder. She smiled and hugged him. He hugged her back.

"Stay safe out there man. Keep a lookout," Mark wished for Quinton.

"You got it," Quinton bumped Mark's fist.

The one who seemed to not be getting any concern was Lenard. He sat alone a short distance from Hamon. He took notice of Lenard and approached him.

"Are you going to say goodbye to anyone?" Hamon asked.

Lenard shook his head, "Nah…I hate goodbyes. I'll just come back, no goodbyes needed."

Hamon wrapped his arm around Lenard, "Are you sure, this might be the last time you see anyone. It's good to at least make sure you give everyone a proper goodbye."

"No thanks," Lenard waved, then removed himself from Hamon's grasp. Amber scooched toward Lenard.

"Stay safe out there you two. Don't you dare get lost out there. And try not to get hurt," She demanded.

Lenard smirked, "Don't worry. I won't get too hurt."

"Hamon…please keep an eye out for everyone. I'm still worried about Kaylee going with you guys," She placed with her hands grasped together.

"I'll keep Kaylee as safe as I possibly can. Lenard will too," Hamon placed his hands over hers.

Amber exhaled, "I know…but watch out for yourself as well. Don't overdo it."

"Thank you, I'll keep that in mind." Amber nodded as she turned away.

"Venturers!" Hamon yelled out. The sounds of voices saying their goodbyes died out. "It's time to get going!" the venturers nodded as they all lined up with Hamon. Hamon stood in the center. Next to him on one side was Lenard and the other was Picc. Next to Lenard was Kaylee.

Hamon stepped in front of the lined group, "Are you all ready!?" they nodded. "If you want to turn back now, now's your chance to do it! Do any of you wish to stay here?!" All of them shook their heads from side to side. "Alright then, say your final goodbyes now!"

The venturers waved their hands toward the rest of the group standing a short distance from them. The rest of the group shouted goodbye toward them.

"Good, now let's get going," Hamon stepped in between the venturers and walked straight toward *The Forest.* The rest of the venturers followed suit directly behind him. As they walked the goodbyes from the main group slowly became echoes. Eventually all became silent.

The light from the campsite faded as well. The only light they possessed now was from the torch Hamon carried.
They hadn't made it that far outside the camp when Picc broke the silence, "How is your visibility? Are you able to see as well as I described?"

"Uhh…I think so…I don't know how it compares to other people really," Kaylee shrugged as she bit her lip.

"Makes sense. I'm sure we'll be able to tell the difference more when we start coming across some camps. How long does it take you to find a campsite anyway?" Picc asked Hamon.

"As it's been lately. A couple hours, maybe even more. Once we get further out we should come across camps more frequently. One thing I have been meaning to ask you. What exactly does this musket look like anyway?" Hamon explained.

"It will have a similar design to the pistol," Picc pulled out the pistol from his pocket and demonstrated it to him. "The only difference is it will have a longer barrel and a slightly longer handle as well. You'll know exactly what I am talking about once we find it."

"Hey, look over there," Kaylee announced as she pointed her finger to something in the distance.

Hamon could not see it. "What is it?" He asked as he looked down the direction Kaylee's finger was pointing.

"Don't you see it? There's a fire." Hamon squinted but only found darkness in that direction.

"That doesn't make sense. There shouldn't be any fires this close to camp," Lenard mentioned.

"No fires that you've spotted yet. That's the benefit of having someone with blue eyes on your side," Picc patted Kaylee's back. She gave him a shaky smile.

"Kaylee…we can't see what you're pointing at. Can you lead us to it?" Hamon requested.

"Uh…sure," Kaylee shrugged as she took the lead in the group. The rest of them followed her. As she led them some of the other members slowly began to take notice of the little glimmer of orange light several hundred feet away. When Hamon took notice of the fire he took the lead of the group once more.

"Are you certain this isn't a campsite you've been to before?" Picc asked.

"We put out the fires of campsites that we've pillaged. For that reason specifically," Quinton explained.

The group arrived at the camp. It seemed to be untampered with. There was one campfire. Three tents surrounded it. Not the largest camp he has come across.

"Lenard, Quinton, find what you can in the tents," he gestured toward the tents. "Kaylee," he glanced at her. "You'll help me scope around the ground."

The group nodded. Lenard and Quinton went off to two different tents. Kaylee searched the ground on the opposite side that he was. The torch he held made it easier to see the objects that laid upon the ground. It was smaller loot, like MREs and even a pocketknife.

Hamon approached her, "Find anything useful?" He asked. "Nothing much. Just a flask and some rope. Total junk," she shrugged.

Hamon smiled, "Makes sense. We typically have to search through a couple camps before we find anything useful or interesting."

Kaylee nodded. The group searched the camp for a while longer. Once they had finished searching they rounded all their items into a small pile. Hamon gazed upon the pile and recited the items in his head. Six MREs, three flasks, rope, a pocketknife, a sock, a shirt and a shovel.

"Who's carrying what?" Quinton asked as he gestured toward the group.

"Lenard can carry the shovel since he has no weapons on him," Hamon waved his hand at him. "Quinton, you'll carry everything else for now. We'll split the supplies up more once we've found more loot," he instructed.

"What about the tents? Do you think we should bring back one or two of them?" Quinton questioned as he glanced back at the small tents.

Hamon shook his head, "They take up too much space. We've got enough tents back at the campsite."

Quinton crumpled his lip, "Are you sure? We're already up to two people per tent and now we have Picc to deal with."

"We'll see about taking a tent back…but we'll load up on supplies first, that's our number one concern here."

Quinton nodded and handed the shovel to Lenard. He packed the rest of the supplies into his backpack. The group put out the fire and took off back into *The Forest*.

They came across several other campsites that Kaylee could not help but to not in her own head. These camps contained materials such as tools, food, water, clothing. Each camp was distraught in its own way. Some seemed to be completely abandoned. No signs of struggle. As if the people who were once there seemed to get up and leave one day.

Other camps were in shreds. The tents were ripped apart. The campfires were in disarray. Shredded clothes scattered the ground. Clear signs that whoever once lived here did not go out in peace. To the venturers, this was nothing but standard. To her, who had only now got to experience *The Forest*, each camp ignited her curiosity.

Thoughts and ideas of what could have happened to these people swelled her mind. It overwhelmed her. Hamon must have noticed this when she was not fully conscious during one of their pillages of the day.

"Are you doing alright?" Hamon asked her while she scanned the ground. His question startled Kaylee out of her trance.

"Uh…w-what?" Kaylee questioned.

Hamon smirked, "I asked if you're alright."

"Oh…uhh yeah," she nodded with a quiver in her lip.

"You're not regretting coming with us now, are you?" Hamon chuckled.

"No! I just…I don't know. It's weird seeing all these torn up camps. I know we are always under threat of attack. But something about these camps…it makes it feel more real. There used to be people here…" She uttered.

"It's something you get used to. Especially when you've dealt with your own monster attacks. It's fine to think but don't get lost in thought. That's how these camps ended up like this," Hamon gestured toward the torn up tent.

"What about the empty camps that are still intact? Why do you think they are like that?" Kaylee asked.

Hamon's hand fell to the back of his head, "It's likely the venturers there decided it was no longer safe. Maybe they saw a monster and booked it. It's hard to tell. There are things out here Klyde and I can't even explain."

Lenard and Quinton exited from the torn up tent. Hamon turned toward them, "Did you find anything?"

Lenard scoffed, "Not a damn thing. Place is empty."

Hamon nodded, "Why don't we rest here for a while. We'll pick back up after a couple of hours."

"Are you sure? We've only pillaged half a dozen camps. It could be hundreds of camps before we find that musket," Picc worried.

"There's no point in overexerting ourselves," Hamon gestured to the other members, "Besides we've got Kaylee with us, she can keep up like we can."

"I'm fine, I can keep going," Kaylee stated.

"No, you can't. Everybody lay down your bags and pick a spot," Hamon turned his gaze away from her. A slight bit of agitation flowed through her chest.

Lenard chose to hunker down near the torn tent. Quinton settled at a tree at the edge of the camp. Picc chose to sit right at the fire. Kaylee was not too far from him. Hamon sat himself next to Kaylee.

The two of them sat in silence for a long moment. The both of them gazed into the fire admiring its warm glow and memorizing pattern.

Kaylee saw Hamon turn his sight to her, and shot her a smile, "you did good today, kid." He patted her back.

Kaylee jolted in place, then turned her head toward him, "oh…thank you."

"I mean it," he raised his forearms. "You did a great job pointing out those campfires to us." He wrapped his arm around her shoulder.

She smiled and let out a little chuckle, "I appreciate it. I'm just happy I could be of help. I'm sorry I got distracted though," she apologized.

Hamon rolled his eyes with a grin, "Don't worry about that. That's what you've got a team for. That's also why we're taking a break."

"I'm not slowing you guys down, am I?" She asked while she bit her lip and clenched her fists. A worry that plagued her mind for some time now.

Hamon sighed, "If I'm being honest…yes. But that's not your fault. It's your first expedition. Lenard and Quinton still slow me down from time to time."

"You've been venturing for a long time right? Longer than my dad?" She asked.

"I started much younger than your dad," Hamon spun his hand. "But in overall years of experience he has me beat."

Kaylee scrunched her lip and placed her hand on her chin, "How old were you when you started?"

"I started when I was fourteen. Four years younger than you were," Hamon said.

Kaylee's mouth gaped and her gaze expanded, "Why did you give me such a hard time starting then?"

"Because you deserve better than that. The group I used to be with was falling into ruin by the time Lenard and I were a part of it," Hamon said.

She felt a little upset that Hamon thought she wasn't capable of dealing with harshness, she also felt a tad of appreciation. It's part of what made her care about him and Lenard so much. "Lenard was a part of your old group?" She asked.

Hamon leaned his head back and put his gaze upward, "Yes, he was. I've known Lenard longer than anyone else has."

"Then do you know why he seems to be pessimistic all the time?" A glare formed on her face as she stared at the trunk Lenard slept at.

Hamon let out an exhale as his gaze fell back onto Kaylee, "He's not pessimistic, he's worried. Lenard was on his own for years before he found my old group. Not even I can imagine what that was like. I get scared of being out on my own just to go take a piss."

"He was on his own for that long?" She asked him in a loud whisper. She had heard tales from her father of people who had gone near mad with fear for having been alone in the forest for just a couple of hours. Lenard being out there for years, she could only imagine the fear and torment.

"Yep," he nodded. "Needless to say, he's attached to people. He has a deeper care for anyone that I know. He also understands *The Forest* like no one else does," Hamon gazed out into the abyss.

"He knows the primal fear of it to a degree I can't even imagine. When you understand that you can't blame him for thinking *The Forest* is something you get into and get out of and nothing more."

"I guess so." Kaylee shrugged.

"Why are you only now asking about all this?" waved his left forearm. "I figured you would have asked me this much sooner knowing you," Hamon questioned.

Kaylee's gaze fell downward, "I…I was worried that I would be prying. I didn't think you would appreciate a question about your past," All she heard from before were small whispers from her father. "From what people tell me, you don't really like to talk about it."

"Really?...Well, I guess I do. It's not exactly fun thinking back on all of that." Kaylee nodded. The two of them remained silent once more. Staring into the fire like they were before.

She glanced back at him, "Do you really think the musket is out there?" Kaylee interrupted.

"Huh?" he arched an eyebrow.

"the musket…do you think we can find it?" She repeated.

"Oh…uhh…I don't know. It's hard to say really. One side of me says that there's no way something like that exists. The other side says that I don't know everything. Who knows really, the only way we'll find out is if we find it."

"Right…I think I'm going to go to sleep now. Thanks for talking with me," Kaylee expressed.

"No problem kid, get some rest," Hamon smiled.

Kaylee got up and rested herself at a tree on the other side of the campfire.

Hamon watched Kaylee as she slept. He began to feel tired himself, however he could not let himself rest as he needed to keep looking out over the camp. Picc rested on the tree closest to the fire, and he noticed that he was also awake. He remained alert and active. As if the travel did not seem to affect his endurance at all.

"What's up with you?" Hamon asked Picc.

Picc gazed at Hamon with his eyes squinted, "What do you mean?" He questioned.

"You don't seem to be tired, not even a bit," Hamon said.

"Oh…I don't get tired very often. A little trait of mine. It's a condition that I have."

He raised his eyebrow, "Condition?"

"Some people have conditions that make them operate differently. I have a condition where I only need a handful of hours of sleep to feel fully rested," he placed his hand on his chest.

"Really? Something you found out from the other world?" Hamon asked.

Picc shook his head, "No actually, I got the name of it from the other world, but not the conditions themselves. I learned it from someone from my old group. He had a condition that made him unable to see, they call it being blind in the other world."

"A condition that doesn't let him see? Nothing at all?" Hamon questioned.

"His eyes didn't function," Picc pointed toward his own eyes. "He said it was a condition he dealt with all his life."

"He mustn't have lasted long then," Hamon said.

"You'd think. But not being able to see seemed to have boosted his hearing ability. The same way Kaylee could see things far before we could, he could hear things. He could hear branches snapping, In a way his abilities were even better than Kaylee's. Since he didn't require some sort of light source for his abilities, unlike Kaylee," Picc said.

"You seem to think very highly of him. Is that just because of his 'abilities.'" Hamon glared at him.

"His blindness did fascinate me. However, he was also a good friend. I was the only one who seemed to think of something more than a liability. They never really took value in my ability either. I tried countless times to work with them, but it never worked," Picc claimed.

Hamon understood very well what it was like to be undermined. His experiences with his old group, while not all negative, were not pleasant either. He had countless stories of how his value would only be used and not appreciated. Something he's received and grown fond of from his current group.

"I know you don't like me very much, but when I admire people's abilities, it's not just for their use. It's for how useful someone can be, I appreciate and respect the amount those people can accomplish," Picc said while he spun his hand.

"I'll keep that in mind," Hamon raised his hand over his mouth and yawned. A small little tear formed in his eye.

"You seem tired. Why don't you get some rest, I'll watch over the camp," Picc offered.

Hamon smirked, "I don't trust you that much. Mind your own business anyway, I've stayed on lookout when I was far more tired than this."

"I'll keep that in mind," Picc repeated.

Several hours later, Lenard stood up from his resting spot and into Hamon's view. He raised his hand in the air and stretched his body. A small groan echoed from him while he did.

Hamon glanced at him, "Sleep well?"

Lenard sneered, "As well as I could. Should I wake the others?" Lenard asked.

"In a bit, we'll let them rest for a tad longer."

"What's up with you? It's not like you to be so easy on everyone," Lenard gestured his hand at him.

Hamon rubbed the back of his head, "Well, we got Kaylee here. That changes things, we can't go as fast as we like."

"I got it," Lenard nodded as he turned his gaze over to Picc. Picc too met his eyes as he gave Lenard a simple smile. Lenard only stared in return.

"How was it staying up with this guy?" He gestured toward Picc.

"Not as bad as you think," Hamon responded. Lenard sat next to Hamon on the same tree.

Lenard snickered, "You are far more tolerant than I. How do you think Kaylee is holding out?"

Hamon gazed at Kaylee. She was slumped over a tree with her mouth slightly opened. He smiled at her, "She's a trooper. She's trying to keep herself from falling behind. But I can tell *The Forest* is getting to her bit by bit."

Lenard placed his hands on his hips, "Do you think she'll make it the full five days?"

"It's only been one day so far and she's only now starting to show signs of being worn out. If she can try to keep ahead throughout our entire journey as she was for this first bit, she'll probably make it," Hamon said.

"And what if she doesn't?" Lenard asked.

Hamon sighed, "We'll have no choice but to turn around and head home. The tricky part is Kaylee isn't going to like that idea very much."

"I wouldn't imagine she would. But regardless that's the right call. I'll take her back myself if you need me to," Lenard claimed.

"No, that's alright. I'd be far too distracted worrying about Kaylee getting back home safely to focus on venturing," Hamon laughed.

Lenard let out a chuckle, "I understand. I'm still not overly fond of her being out here with us."

"I don't think any of us are," Hamon said.

"It's just..." Lenard clenched his fists, "A kid like her shouldn't be out here. I was hoping coming out here might teach her what kind of place *The Forest* really is. It doesn't look like her spirited self is worn out at all though."

"That's how Kaylee is," he smiled as he glanced back at her for a moment.

Lenard chuckled, "That's what got me worried. She doesn't understand *The Forest* isn't some challenge to be conquered. Have I...Have I ever told you about the breathing story?"

Hamon squinted, "No, I don't think you have."

"It's a story from back when I was out on my own. I was resting at an abandoned camp for the night. I was all tired out from running away from a monster I thought I had heard. I was sitting there at the fire. In that sickening silence. Nothing but the cracking of flames.

Well, I wasn't too familiar with keeping a fire lit nor did I have any tools to use to keep it lit. It was a cycle of me staying at a campfire until it went out then going to the next one. Anyway, I was up for a very long time.

The fire was resting at its last embers. I stared at it as I slowly watched the glowing red patches of fire attached to the wood die out. The cracking of the fire had disappeared. I was talking to myself, tapping my foot on the ground just to hear something.

Then…I hear breathing. It was deep and slow, almost calming. It sounded as if whatever was breathing was doing so from multiple mouths. I was frightened that it might have been a monster, but I never once ever heard a monster…breath.

I thought then it could be another venturer. Maybe they didn't know I was there. So I called out. I heard nothing in response, only more breathing. But something felt off. I closed my eyes so I could hear better.

That's when a shiver was sent down my spine. The breathing wasn't coming from around me, not from the front or back. I heard the breathing from *above.* I panicked so hard I got up and ran the instant I found that out. I eventually found another camp, and never heard the breathing again."

"Are you sure you weren't imagining the whole thing?" Hamon proposed.

Lenard groaned as he gazed into the void, "I could have been…but it felt so real. I'm not the only one that's experienced something like that."

Hamon nodded. The haunting feeling of *The Forest.* That strange feeling of being alone, yet not at the same time. A feeling that could drive someone insane.

"Right…we should get going," Hamon stated as he stood up.

"Not going to get any rest yourself?" Lenard asked.

"I don't need it," Hamon stood upright and turned back to Lenard.

"If you say so," Lenard shrugged as he stood up along with Hamon. "I'll go wake everyone up."

Chapter 6

Creeping

A fire blurred in front of Lenard. His head felt fuzzy. Like he wasn't quite awake, in some sort of dream. He rubbed his eyes. The flame came into full focus. The fire was not far from him. Attached to the fire was a stick. His eyes fell down the stick that held the fire into the air, where a hand was at the bottom.

He analyzed it. The hand belonged to someone who had brown hair, muscular stature. He had a sense of familiarity. However, who this was did not quite cross his mind. He took his gaze off the man and looked to the man he noticed next to the torch holder. He was blonde, shorter in height but bigger in muscle.

He was talking to the torch holder. But all he could hear were mumbles as the blonde man's arms made different gestures. The blonde man too had a sense of familiarity. However, he also felt a sense of nostalgia wash over him when he saw the blonde man.

Like these were people he had known for years yet hadn't seen in the same amount of years. Then, he felt an arm land on his shoulder.

"You aren't getting tired are you?" Lenard looked toward the man who placed his hand on his shoulder. Another man, this time with black, short, spiky hair. He wore a black jacket and a smug smile whipped his face. Lenard knew this man, he couldn't remember his name, but he knew him. A lost memory on the tip of his tongue.

"I'm fine," he responded.

The black haired man smirked. "Well you better not cause us any problems." He stepped ahead of him. Lenard was now at the back of the group. Everything came into view now. They walked through *The Forest.* He could not remember why but he knew the reason was probably for food or water.

His feeling of dizziness disappeared, yet he still could not recall these people. He couldn't shake the feeling that he was missing something. He knew these people yet he didn't.

The group of venturers arrived at an abandoned campsite. The tents were torn. Weapons were broken. *Blood* spilled across the ground.

"Sorry fuckers…must have gotten jumped," The black hair man remarked.

Lenard stood there. He felt a sense of sorrow for these people. What happened to them? Why them? Who did this to them? *What* did this to them? He couldn't help but feel sorry for the people who just tried to survive. Were there children here? Women? Innocent young men? It overwhelmed him.

"Everyone! Search for anything we can use!" The torch holder instructed. Lenard took his gaze off of the blood on the ground. The members of the group began to analyze the camp for supplies.

Lenard followed them and tried his best to stay focused on finding anything. Whenever he came across blood a sense of panic would come back to strike him. The blonde man must have noticed this and approached him.

"Are you okay? Is this your first time seeing blood?" He asked. Unlike the black haired man, he seemed to be concerned for his wellbeing. Lenard looked toward him as he gave a shaky nod. He knew this person, he was his friend. What was his name?…Marvin, it was Marvin. He called him Marv for short.

"I'm only a bit tired. I promise," he lied. Marvin gave him a look that told him he knew he was lying.

"Don't overwork yourself. We can always head back to camp if we need to." Lenard nodded. Marvin stepped away and went back to surveying. He sighed as he continued his search as well. On the ground he found a metal flask surrounded by a puddle of water. He picked it up and analyzed it. A tear down near the bottom of the flask emptied out all of the water.

The brown haired man stood near the fire, "Any of you find anything?"

"Nothing, you'd think a camp like this would have loads of stuff," the black haired man complained.

"What should we do?" Marvin asked the torch holder.

"We'll keep venturing, we don't have enough supplies to go home yet," The brown-haired man said.

"Are you sure that's a good idea? I don't think we have enough pebbles to mark our path to make it to another camp," Marvin said.

"Not like we have a choice," The black haired man's voice boomed.

The black haired man placed his hand on Marvin's shoulder, "Maybe we should put more consideration into it. We've been exploring for nearly three days. We're beginning to get worn out. If we aren't careful, a monster attack could be the end of us."

"We can handle a monster attack. What we can't handle is another week of starvation." The mens' arguing slowly faded to muffles. He looked off into the distance. Out into the darkness beyond the fire. He felt himself grow unconscious. He still had felt as if he was not all there and was unsure of why.

As the mens' talking continued to muffle more and more, he heard something. It sounded like footsteps far in the distance. Thud after thud, but something was wrong.

The footsteps didn't sound human. In fact, it sounded more like footsteps of that of a monster, but even that didn't fit. They were too *big*. The thuds were far too loud for how far they seemed to be away. There were also too many. Like whatever walked had several dozens of legs that thumped onto the ground. The sound…it almost reminded him of a spider.

He didn't know why. To him…he shouldn't know what a spider sounds like. Yet, that's the only thing he could compare it to. He was frozen in fear and looked off in the distance. He saw *something*.

Almost something he couldn't comprehend. A mass that was darker than pitch black, something he told himself should not be possible. Yet, nonetheless, he could see it. The…*nothingness*.

Its voided body towered several meters above the trees. Its legs angled upwards almost ninety degrees. Before it angled back downwards, and it moved. The nothingness didn't just move...*it approached.* A shock of fear came over Lenard. He turned around back toward his fellow venturers...however, they were gone, vanished.

Not a trace of them left. Except...an object that laid right in front of Lenard. He stepped forward as he picked the object up. It was glasses. Again, he was unsure how he knew that that should be information unfamiliar to him. Yet, he knew it all the same.

The lenses were shattered. The arms were almost chewed. *Blood* tainted them. Then...he heard a noise. A noise that shook him to his very core. A noise he did recognize the instant he heard it.

He prayed that his senses were playing tricks on him. But he could not ignore reality. He closed his eyes to listen. What he heard confirmed his fears. He began to sweat. His breathing grew heavier. The air grew denser.

...He heard breathing from the sky...

"Lenard!" Hamon shouted. Lenard startled upright as he yelped. He awoke in a cold sweat and frantically glanced around. Hamon knelt down next to him. Behind him was Kaylee, Quinton and Picc, who were all ready to continue the venture, with their bags wrapped around their shoulders. No brown haired man, no black haired man, no Marvin. His state of confusion dissipated as he realized his reality.

"What's going on?" Lenard asked.

Hamon raised his eyebrow, "Were leaving...it's the final day of the expedition, remember?"

"Oh yeah...right," He spoke with deep breaths in between.

Hamon laid his hand on his shoulder, "Are you okay? You seem panicked,"

"I'm fine. I just had a nightmare. That's all," in reality, he was not fine. There was still much he was confused about. The dream felt too vivid to be that. Although, it did not feel conscious enough to have really happened.

"Well then get up. We can't lie around here forever," Hamon instructed. Lenard nodded as he took one last deep breath then pushed himself upright. He grabbed his bag that lay next to him and wrapped it around his shoulders.

"Let's get going," Hamon led the group onwards back into *The Forest*. Lenard hung at the end of the group and walked behind them at a slower pace. Kaylee slowed her pace to put herself next to Lenard.

"What was that all about?" She asked.

"What are you talking about?" Lenard questioned.

Kaylee snickered, "You woke up almost screaming. What kind of nightmare were you having?"

Lenard sneered, "Shut it kid."

"I'm not judging," Kaylee raised her hands in a defensive manner. "I get it, I'm only curious to know. If anyone here was going to wake up screaming it was going to be me. So what nightmare were you having?"

"Kid…I don't know. Don't worry about it," he waved her off as a wave of irritation brushed him.

"Sorry, didn't mean to annoy you," she apologized.

"Don't worry about it. It's on me. I don't like being out in *The Forest* for this long. How are you holding up?" It was the last day. All of the venturers were tired out. Lenard had noticed Kaylee growing tired herself. She was quiet from the start but spirited. Now, she was stiff and her body leaked of fatigue. He knew well that they were in no condition to flee from a monster if one were to approach.

"I can handle myself," she lied.

"Good..." Lenard's train of thought wandered off again. He was unaware as to how he knew the names of those items. The one thing he recognized from the dream was that breathing. Lenard picked up his pace up toward the front of the group and positioned himself next to Picc.

"Hey, I have a question for you," Lenard whispered to Picc.

Picc raised his eyebrow, "What is it?"

"Do you know anything about...glasses?"

He raised an eyebrow, "Glasses?"

"Yeah, those," Lenard shrugged.

"Why do you ask?" Picc question with a sly smile.

"Just answer my question," Lenard demanded.

"Yes, I know what glasses are. They're an object from the other world. They were used to help people see better," Picc said.

"Wait...doesn't anything you see from the other world supposed to not exist in this one?" Lenard questioned.

"Yes," Picc stared at him with a suspicious glare, "It makes me curious as to how you know about them."

"I think I saw it in a journal or something," Lenard lied.

"Right," Picc said. He was left even more confused now. Either Picc was being untruthful or something even more mysterious was happening. He could not see a reason as to why Picc would be reserved in this matter.

What left him even more confused was Marvin and the group he was with. Lenard knows he was with no such group. There was his original group, then Hamon's old group, then this one. There was no blonde haired man named Marvin from any of these groups. However, he felt as if he somehow recognized the man. Like he knew him from somewhere he couldn't quite recall.

"There's another campsite ahead!" Kaylee announced. She pointed off into the void. Hamon nodded. Kaylee led the group toward the fire with a short hike.

The fire came into view for Lenard. At the back of the group, he kept his eyes on Hamon. The site of the back of his head. The way he held his torch. It gave a sickening sense of Deja vu. Lenard analyzed the camp when it came into clearer view.

The campsite has two fires and somewhere around five tents. Not too much smaller than their own campsite. Once they arrived at the camp, the group broke into their usual places. Lenard searched the tents with Quinton.

The tents were in perfect order with nothing that seemed to be destroyed or torn. The entire camp was in good shape. A more negative sign. As it means the people of this camp willfully left, therefore must have taken all of their supplies with them.

This was not the case with this camp, however. There were over a dozen MREs and nine flasks of water in just the tents alone. Clothes were scattered across the floor of the tents. Supplies and tools were laid down. It was as if the survivors had fallen asleep, only to disappear the next day. As if they had just vanished. The state of this camp left Lenard with an anxious and paranoid feeling.

He ignored his feelings and scavenged all of the items from the tents anyway. He lined all of the items at the larger fire of the camp. As he did, he kept an eye on Kaylee. Her movements were sluggish and her eyes were tired. Hamon continued his line of items with the supplies he had found on the surrounding ground.

As he knelt down, Lenard whispered to him, "Is it just me or is something not right about this campsite?"

Hamon leaned his head closer to him. "I get what you mean. Let's just get everything we can and get out of here."

Lenard nodded as he organized all of the supplies laid on the ground. After he finished, Hamon called the group toward the larger fire.

"Give us a rundown of the supplies we got," Hamon instructed.

"We got fifteen MREs, twelve flasks of water, two of them are half empty, the rest are full. We got a full pair of clothes along with three extra socks and a jacket. For tools, we got a screwdriver, a miniature hatchet, scissors and twelve feet of rope. Overall, a very good haul, almost too good."

"Then we should cut our losses here. Better to end on a successful pillage," Hamon announced.

Picc scoffed, "No, we should keep going," he said as he crossed his arms.

Hamon turned to him with his hands placed on his hips, "Why is that?"

"The amount of camps we explored. We're not at a good rate. Over these past five days we've explored over twenty camps. We'll have to explore hundreds before we find that musket. At this rate it could take us years to find the musket," Picc stated.

"I understand your concerns. However, you're ignoring everyone here's state of being. Other than myself and you, everyone is tired. We can't venture with our members too tired, a monster attack can be far more lethal that way," Hamon said.

Picc waved his hand in the direction of the abyss, "Then the three of them can head back to camp, you and I can keep venturing."

"That's not going to happen. I have personal responsibility over Kaylee. I'm not going to send her off with members who are almost as tired as she is," Hamon stated.

"I can keep going," Kaylee jolted up right and held her eyes open wide in an unnatural manner.

Hamon shook his head, "No, you can't. You've done really well, but all of us have a limit and you reached yours yesterday. If it takes us years to find the musket because of that, then that's how it's going to have to be."

Quinton interjected himself in the center of the camp, "Maybe we could do one more."

"One more?" Hamon asked.

"Yes, just one more," Quinton held up his index finger, "This campsite was a pretty big haul, we must be far out. We found one more camp out here, it's got to be just as good of a haul as this one."

"Hmm," Hamon laid his finger and thumb on his chin. "I suppose that could work."

"I don't like it, something about these camps isn't right. There's tons of loot left yet nothing is damaged. That doesn't make any sense," Lenard said.

"One more camp shouldn't be the end of us. How about it Picc," Quinton turned to him "Will one more campsite suffice?"

Picc stood still for a moment, "One more camp won't be enough."

"Well, either way we aren't venturing for a significant amount of time. We either do one more camp or none at all," Hamon said.

Picc sighed, "Fine…I suppose one more camp will at least bring us closer."

"Then it's settled. One more camp and then we head back. Any complaints?" The group of venturers all shook their heads.

"Then let's get a move on," Hamon led the group toward the voided woods. All other venturers other than himself and Picc were tired out. He was surprised Picc was able to keep up with him.

For an *Appearer*, he made a great venturer. It took Hamon decades to get as good as he is. Picc's lack of fatigue could be due to his…condition. However, that wouldn't explain how his body itself did not experience fatigue.

Something about Picc did not seem right to him. Something about this entire venture did not feel right. During the five days they had ventured, not a single monster attack had occurred.

Monster attacks are rare, but five days out in *The Forest* should have been enough to come across at least one monster.

The closest they have come was the time Kaylee stated that she noticed something that moved, halfway into the second day. The venturers fled as soon as she claimed this. They should have run into more monsters than that.

It left him with an uneasy feeling. Almost as if something had been plotting how to kill them. The others did not seem to be bothered by this, as they lacked the experience he had with *The Forest.* Each step they took further into *The Forest* caused his paranoia to grow.

"I see a fire," Kaylee announced.

Hamon snapped out of thought and glanced at her. "Where?" He asked.

They followed the same routine, Kaylee led the adventures to the fire. This campsite had one massive fire surrounded by four tents. Same as the other, there was no noticeable damage to the tents.

The paranoia he felt spiked. He felt as if they should turn back. As if they had made a mistake to step foot in that camp. It was agreed to pillage one more camp however, and he knew better than to go back on an agreement.

"Let's get this over with," Hamon ushered. The venturers nodded as they spread across the camp. He cautiously searched the ground and felt himself getting distracted as he frequently peeked his eyesight upward from the ground.

"Hey, I think I found something," Kaylee announced. The group peered over to Kaylee. In her hands she held a curved stick, tied to both ends was a string. Along with it was a bag of sticks with points of iron.

Picc slid himself next to Kaylee, "That's a bow, and the bag is a bunch of arrows."

"May I see it?" He asked.

"...Sure," Kaylee handed the bow and arrows to him.

"You use the tight string of the bow to launch an arrow at high speeds. I've seen someone from my previous group use one before. They're not quite as rare as a pistol, but not as good either. Let me see if I can use it."

Picc grabbed one of the arrows out of the bag. He struggled to line the arrow with the string of the bow. He pulled the arrow back with the string. The wooden ends of the bow ached as they were stretched. Picc released the arrow from his two fingers and it zoomed. It flew out into the distance.

Picc and Kaylee looked in the direction of the arrow. The tents blocked Quinton, Lenard and Hamon from seeing in that direction. All they saw was Kaylee's face of fascination. However…her face morphed and became fearful. Picc looked concerned as well.

"What's wrong?" Kaylee did not speak, her eyes were widened, her forehead sweaty, her movements were panicked.

All she could muster was to point at whatever she was looking at. Hamon and Lenard hurried over to see what it was.

At the edge of the camp was a woman with black hair that flowed to her chest out of sight. Her back was turned to them and she was naked. She made no movements as she stood still.

"Ma'am?" Hamon called out. The woman did not respond nor move. Lenard cautiously approached her.

"Ma'am?! Are you okay? We're venturers, we can help you if you need." Kaylee grasped onto Hamon's shoulder. She whispered something incoherent.

He knelt down closer to Kaylee leaned toward his ear. Another incoherent whisper. “What was that?’ He asked.

“That thing…it isn’t human,” She whispered. A chill shivered down Hamon’s spine.

“Lenard! Get away!” He shouted. Lenard stumbled backward, almost tripping over himself.

“Picc, shoot it! Shoot it now!” Hamon commanded. Picc sheathed his pistol from his hip and aimed the gun toward the woman.

“Take the shot!” Picc nodded as he pulled the trigger. A flash of light followed by a loud bang echoed through the trees. The light died down and the woman came back into view.

A pellet sized hole was left on the middle of her spine. An injury that would make a normal human limp. However, the woman was unmoved. Blood poured from the hole as it leaked down her body. He stood there and feared that his next move may be his last.

Kaylee shivered and shook. He felt her erratic movement pressed against his shoulder. She saw the monster for what it truly was and could see what lied beyond the woman. What rested right outside of the void he could not see.

A low growl could be heard just beyond the woman. The still woman’s body twitched. Its first sign of movement. The body rose into the air off of its feet. Blood dripped down from the legs. The flesh of the woman grew darker as it faded into the void. In its place, two white eyes glared at the venturers.

“Picc…reload the gun,” Hamon whispered. Picc pulled out the small baggie of pellets. As he did, the monster placed its claw in view of the fire.

"Hurry up!" Hamon panicked as the monster clawed its way out of the void. Half of the body of the monster was in view. It sprawled its arm outwards. Picc hastened his pace, opened the baggie, and placed a pellet into the barrel. He was able to see that Picc would not have enough time.

"Everybody, run!!" He shouted. He grabbed Kaylee's arm as he turned his back toward the monster. He sprinted away with Kaylee in reach and prayed that the others had the sense to run as well. They sprinted past the edge of the fire as they once more entered the darkness.

The torch Hamon held in his other hand lit the way. Beside him he noticed Lenard, who followed close in suit. What if the others?

What kind of monster was that? What kind of monster was able to trick? All these thoughts that ran through Hamon's head as he sprinted. Then he heard the pounding of the monster's claws as it chased after them.

He knew there was no hope of out running this beast, so he came to a halt as he turned and positioned Kaylee behind him. The monster towered over him. He let go of Kaylee's hand and retrieved his hatchet. The monster swiped down at him.

He sliced the monster's hand as it crashed down on him. It retracted its claw in pain, then growled at him. He readied his hatchet for another blow. Instead of attacking, the monster stuck out its tail in front of him. At the end of the tail was the woman attached to its tail like it was a part of it.

He allowed himself to get distracted by its rise and it clawed at him from his left. The impact bashed Hamon's rib cage. He was sent flying until he crashed into a tree to his side.

The torch he held landed on the ground next to him. Lenard placed himself in front of Kaylee.

The monster towered over him as well. Its claw came crashing down. Lenard was flung to the ground under the weight. Dirt particles spurted upwards as Lenard connected to the ground. It focused its attention on Kaylee. It towered over her and she trembled. Sweat dripped down her forehead and she stepped backward in a panicked motion.

"Kaylee!" Hamon shouted as blood spat from his mouth. She took another shaky step backward and the monster gave a deep growl as it raised its arm. Kaylee screamed as she turned her back and ran.

"Kaylee!" Hamon called out once more. The monster ignored him and chased after her. Its body disappeared from the range of light as it ran after her.

The pounding claws and Kaylee's panicked screaming could be heard slowly peering off into the distance. Hamon picked himself off of the ground. Bones made a cracking noise as he did.

He groaned in pain and the torch off of the ground. He limped toward the sound of Kaylee's screaming. Each step he took he groaned once again in pain.

He ignored the pain as he continued forth toward Kaylee's direction. A dread filled emotion came over him as her screaming dulled out. He picked up the pace knowing the damage he may be doing to his own body.

The screaming faded out to the point where it was too far to tell its direction. Hamon collapsed to the ground. His leg felt like it was broken. The torch fell next to him and he placed his hand outward. He clutched the ground as he dragged his limp body forward.

The screaming faded more, until all noise died out and there was nothing but echoes once more. The groans of Lenard and the crackles of fire was all he could hear now.

Chapter 7

Lost

Lenard awoke sat at a tree with blurred vision that felt familiar. He gazed at a campfire that rested in front of him and placed his hand over his forehead. His eyes were covered from the fire as a result.

He groaned as he placed his other hand on the trunk of the tree and used his hand as support to stand. He set the tips of his two fingers on the lids of his eyes and rubbed his eyes to satisfaction, then opened them. All was a blur for a brief moment, then everything came into focus.

Across the fire were two men, the brown and black haired men he saw before. The brown-haired man noticed Lenard, "You're awake. That's good, we're getting back on the move soon." His voice was deep, and somewhat intimidating.

"You think next camp we pillage we'll find it?" The black-haired man asked Lenard.

Lenard groaned, "Uhh…find what again?"

The black haired man burrowed his eyebrows, "The musket? The thing you've been telling us about."

The musket? "Uhh…right, sorry. I guess my rest scrambled my memory," He lied. The black-haired man said he was leading them to the musket, or whoever he was right now. He remembered now, this dream he had, but what could it be, not anything from him.

He did not know these people. The sense of familiarity he had with them was not his own either. If he was the one leading them toward the musket in this dream, does that mean this is Picc's memories? It could be the only explanation.

That left him with an even bigger and more confusing question. How? How could any of this be happening? This shouldn't be possible and yet it was.

A hand landed on his shoulder, "Are you alright?"

Lenard turned backward to see Marvin, "Oh…yeah. I just…don't feel like I know what's going on right now."

Marvin snickered, "I get what you mean. Maybe a couple of more searches and we'll find that musket. Only time could tell."

"I guess so. How much longer are we going to be out here?" Lenard asked as he picked himself off the ground. His legs ached and a groan left his mouth.

Marvin shook his head with a smile, "Who knows, maybe a couple more days…maybe a couple more weeks. The captain is pretty set on finding the rifle. You really set him off by telling him about it. I've never seen him this passionate about something."

"Right…and if you don't mind, can you remind me of what the captain's name is?" He asked.

"Oh, you've probably only heard us referring to him as that. I forget that you're new here. The captain's name is Gunther," Marvin said.

He pointed toward the black haired man, "Over there is Klein, in case you didn't know his name either."

"Yeah, thanks." He leaned against the tree behind him and analyzed the campsite.

There was one tent, and next to it was an opened duffle bag with the handle of a shovel sticking out. The camp smelled of ash and heated MREs. The captain and Klein were talking about something.

Despite being within hearing distance of Lenard all he heard were mumbles. Even the crackling of the fire and Marvin's voice was muffled. He was aware, yet his senses were dulled. A feeling similar to what someone feels right as they wake up. However, he felt awake.

"I think we'll be heading back to camp soon," Marvin said.

He glanced at him, "Will we?"

Marvin stretched his lips, "I believe so, I don't think we could hold onto anymore stuff, our bags would burst."

He noticed the bags that were scattered across the campsite. Each one filled to the brim with what he concluded was water, tools, food and clothing.

He turned to Marvin, "Weren't you saying the Captain wanted to keep going for the musket?"

"Yeah…but he'll come to realize we can't go on forever. Especially with that monster lurking around," Marvin said.

Lenard nodded. He felt a paranoid feeling strike his chest. Memories from the last time he experienced this flooded into his head. He remembered the blood, void and…the glasses.

"Hey, this is going to seem like a weird question, but is there a member at the campsite who has glasses?" He asked.

Marvin squinted, "Uhhh…yep. I forget what his name is, he's newer here. I don't know why but he gives me the creeps. I thought you had talked with him before. Why do you ask?"

"I…I'm not sure yet." He had a feeling that for whatever reason he was having these dreams, the man in glasses had something to do with it.

He was not quite sure yet, but he was certain that if he possessed those very same glasses he saw, then this wasn't a coincidence. Although whatever he was experiencing seemed and felt like a dream, he suspected that it wasn't, but had nothing more than a sneaking suspicion about it. "What about that blood-ridden camp we found? What happened after you guys went off?"

Marvin squinted, "What are you talking about? What blood-ridden camp?"

"The one we were at? The tents were torn, blood all over the place?" Marvin looked more confused.

"I think I would remember that. I've never been to a camp ridden in blood." Now Lenard squinted. He's in some sort of dreamscape and the last time he was in this state was an event that has not happened.

How could an event not have happened yet still be real. Maybe, if these are Picc's memories, then this could be a memory further into the past.

That would make sense. Since Marvin hinted that they may have been venturing for weeks in the future memory. In this current one, Picc has only been a part of this group for a couple weeks at most.

The pieces were starting to come together. The only questions that remained in Lenard's mind were How is this happening? As Well as…why him?

The captain stood up and for the first time since he's entered this current dreamscape the captain was in full focus. No longer blurred from his vision.

"Grab your bags, we're heading back to the camp now," He instructed.

Marvin leaned in, "See."

"Yes," Lenard nodded, grabbed the nearest bag, and wrapped it around his shoulders. The captain grabbed the torch that was set next to the campfire. Lenard lined up together with the rest of the group as they ventured back into the forest.

The warm glow from the campfire slowly faded away. Lenard, at the back of the group, turned backwards as the fire grew blurrier.

Within the same view of that blurry fire was a new light within Lenard's vision. Still blurry, he squinted his eyes. It was a torch no more than a dozen feet away from him. To the right of his vision was the grassy dirt floor of *The Forest* that his right cheek rested on.

The smell of dirt he lied on bathed his nose, then the smell of blood. Concerned, he positioned his arm to lift him and stood upwards. His legs were shaky and groaned as he stood upright.

"Lenard." His name startled him and he looked toward his right where the noise came from. Upon the ground was Hamon.

He rested his back on a tree and was clutching his right rib cage with his other hand placed in his leg.

Blood dripped from his mouth. The dark stain on the rib Hamon was grasping was too far for him to tell if it was blood or dirt. He could not quite remember what was happening. "Hamon?" He whispered. "Wha…what's going on?"

"Kay…Kaylee…she's missing," Hamon gazed down to the ground.

"What?…" He took shaky steps toward him.

"The monster chased after her, we don't know where she went." The voice came from his side, he turned to see Quinton with a look of despair plastered on his face.

Lenard rushed to him and grabbed him by the collar, "What do you mean you don't know where she went? Why weren't you following her!"

"Hamon, Quinton and yourself were injured. I stayed behind to ensure none of you were killed." Next to Quinton, rested on a tree same as Hamon, was Picc. He gazed off into the distance and did not even bother to look him in the eyes.

"And why the hell are you so relaxed?" He asked as he let go of Quinton.

Picc sighed, "There hasn't been any sign of monsters around besides that one."

"Tsk…we should be out there looking for Kaylee." Lenard turned to the open abyss and prepared to walk down into it.

"With all due respect. None of us are in any condition to look for her. Besides, if she is still alive, it's wisest to remain here. Moving from this location not only puts us in danger, but what if Kaylee were to find her way back here and we weren't here. Staying here is the correct option," Picc said.

Lenard sneered in Picc's direction, "I don't give a damn what you think. You don't even look the slightest bit concerned for her!"

"Why should I…it's not like I knew her very well," Picc claimed.

He saw red and lunged toward Picc. Quinton grabbed onto him and held him back before he could do anything. Picc remained rested, unphased and now looked Lenard in the eyes.

"Calm down," Quinton demanded as shoved him away. Lenard scoffed and kept his distance.

"He has a point.," Quinton gestured at Picc. "You know I care about Kaylee, but if we rush out there then we will not be helping anyone."

"I don't care. You can't just expect me to sit here and do nothing while Kaylee is out there! On her own!…oh god," He collapsed back onto the ground. "Fuck…" Tears began to swell in his eyes. "Th…This is your fault…Hamon. You were the one who said she should come. I told you!…I told you bringing her was a bad idea!"

Quinton placed his hand on his chest, "Hey…I was saying she should have come as well-"

"No," Both him and Quinton glanced at Hamon, "he's right. It's my fault. It was my call whether she would come or not. You're not to blame."

Lenard stood up once more, "No…I'm sorry. This is no time to be placing blame. We need to look for her."

"Like I said. The correct option is to wait here," Picc said.

"There's not a shot in hell I'm waiting here. I'm going after her whether or not I have to go alone," he walked toward the edge of the light the torch provided.

"You're letting your emotions get the best of you. Even if you do go off on your own, right now only you and I are capable of standing," Picc gestured toward Lenard, then himself, "I'm not much of a fighter. All you'll be doing is leaving the rest of us in more danger. I understand you would give your life to find Kaylee, but don't be selfish and risk all of ours."

"Enough!" Hamon clutched the tree behind him and used it to move himself upright. "Picc, I understand the reasons why you don't want to look for her, and that you don't have much connection to her. If you wish to leave, you can." A sneer formed from Picc's mouth.

"However, the rest of us are looking for her. It doesn't matter if it's the 'correct' decision or not. Were her team…her family. We will not abandon her out there to fend for herself."

Picc pushed himself off of the tree and stood upright, "That won't work. If all of you go then that means I'll have to travel back to the campsite on my own. In which, I will most certainly collide with a monster."

"Well…you're always welcome to join us," Hamon shrugged.

"Tsk…fine, I guess I have no choice," He rolled his eyes. Hamon retrieved the torch from the ground. "Last I heard the screaming coming from that direction. Quinton, are you able to stand?"

Quinton nodded as he struggled to stand upright, then huddled with the rest of the group. "Let me lay it straight, we are not coming back until we find Kaylee, all of you understand." The group nodded. "Then let's go."

He led the group back into the abyss. They traveled across the noticeable tracks left by the monster. Dirt patches that looked squished, parts of tree trunks that were smashed in. All of these signs helped the group to remain searching.

They called out Kaylee's name every so often. No sounds of the monster, nor any audible screaming from Kaylee. Something Hamon took as both a positive and negative sign.

Picc positioned himself next to Hamon, "You know, following the tracks of the monster is going to lead us to…the monster, not Kaylee. You know that right?"

"I know it's a risk, but a risk is what we need to take right now. Also, I would appreciate some insight on what exactly that thing was," Hamon requested.

Picc shrugged, "No idea, I've never seen it before."

Lenard furrowed his brow, "You? You've never seen that before? Are you absolutely sure?"

"Positive." Lenard glared at him, then gave a slight nod. If in those memories, he really was Picc, then how could he not know of the body decoy monster. The venturers he was with knew about it, was that perhaps not Picc?

Was he in someone else's memories? Maybe he was seeing the future. Lenard dismissed that possibility. If he saw into the future it would be even more ridiculous than seeing Picc's old memories.

He felt that he should perhaps keep it a secret that he was seeing into Picc's supposed past. If that really was what he was seeing. For he had not even confirmed if this was the case. At least he should keep this secret from Picc.

He positioned himself next to Hamon and leaned in close, "I think Picc is hiding something."

Hamon raised an eyebrow, "What makes you think that?"

"He knows something about that monster. I'm sure of it. His whole calm demeanor wouldn't add up anywise," Lenard said.

"That's not a whole lot of proof to go off of. I know you're not trusting of other people, but now is not the time to speculate about these types of things," Hamon claimed.

Lenard let out a small hiss, "I…I know this is going to sound crazy."

"What are you talking about?" Hamon asked.

Lenard glared down at the ground for a moment, then recalled his eyes to Hamon, "I…I think I'm seeing into Picc's memories."

Hamon crumpled his eyebrows and gave him the most concerned look he had ever seen from him.

Lenard raised his hands in a defensive manner, "I know it sounds crazy but hear me out first. When the monster knocked me out, I had a dream with these people I felt I recognized, that said I was helping them find the musket."

Hamon snickered, "Lenard…it sounds like you just had a normal dream. I think you are overthinking it."

Lenard sighed, "I know…but I have this feeling. Like there's something more to it."

"You aren't sounding like yourself. Since when do you think there's deeper meaning to anything? Look, you're tired, that's all there is to it. Besides, even if what you are seeing is…Picc's old memories, that doesn't have anything to do with our current situation," Hamon stated.

Lenard opened his mouth to speak, but to shut it closed. Hamon was right. He had no confirmation of any of this, and even if he did it wouldn't matter.

Regardless of how much he felt there was something more to these dreams, he couldn't prove it. He re-focused his attention on searching for Kaylee and analyzed the ground for any more clues that could help them. On one of the blades of grass, he noticed a tiny dark drop. It was almost impossible to see.

He knelt down. Hamon halted once he noticed, "What is it?" Hamon asked. Lenard reached out his arm and extended two fingers, then wiped whatever the substance was off of the blade of grass.

"It's blood," Lenard said. Hamon's eyes widened.
He clenched his fist, "It's probably from the monster, that means we're on the right track."

"I wouldn't be so confident about that. Monster's don't bleed red blood," Picc noted.

"The hole you put in the body decoy, there was red blood leaking from there," Hamon proposed.

"Then we would have noticed the blood from the beginning. Where the monster was at. It makes no sense why the bleeding would only start now. After a longer period of time," Picc said.

"It doesn't matter who the blood came from. It doesn't change what we have to do," Hamon claimed.

"Right, of course. But I still think it's important that we look at this objectively. If Kaylee really is bleeding, that means we'll need bandages. It also means our time is limited, depending on how badly she's bleeding." Hamon nodded.

Lenard stood upright and the group continued forward. As they carried on, the blood following the path became more noticeable. Drops turned to splatters. Splatters turned to splotches.

Splotches tuned to *puddles*. All the while there was still no sign of Kaylee. No dropped materials or ripped clothing. Not a single noise besides the frantic, shallow breathing of

"*Shit*," Lenard said with a quiver. Hamon glanced over to him. His arms were wrapped around each other and he breathed a shaky and off sync breath, then his eyes widened.

Hamon placed his arm on his shoulder, "We don't know if it's even her blood yet, take it easy."

Lenard nodded as he took a deep breath in and out. Hamon kept his hand placed on his shoulder not just to comfort him, but himself as well.

The signs of smashed dirt and pushed in trees had vanished. The only sign remaining being the blood. The trail led to the entrance of a small cave. The venturers stopped right outside of it.

"Kaylee!" Hamon shouted into the shaft, his own echoed voice was all that returned. Quinton searched for any other areas the trail might have gone. There was nothing, however.

"I don't think it's wise to go in there," Picc said.

Hamon sighed, "We don't have a choice. Kaylee could be unconscious down there."

"There could also be a monster waiting for us. Maybe only one of us should go down there," Quinton said.

"I'll go down there," he turned around to the members, "The three of you keep watch out. If you hear me screaming, then run, don't even think about coming down yourselves."

Lenard stepped forward, "Are you sure about this? I have more experience being on my own, I'm better suited for this."

"No, I'll do it. I need to take the torch down with me in order to see. I need you here to keep both of them calm," Hamon said. Lenard pursed his lips, then nodded.

He entered the cave. Cold, humid moisture seeped into his skin. It smelled of blood and vomit. A horrid smell even Hamon couldn't help but cringe from.

Drops of water echoed through the chambers, or at least he hoped that it was water. The trail of blood continued and it splattered across the walls. Puddles of blood filled the uneven divots of the floor.

The blood that colored this cave had to have been from dozens of venturers. He arrived at the end of the cave. Somewhere around thirty feet away and six feet down from the entrance. There was a horrifying sight of blood, guts, bones and corpses.

All piled together like some sick piece of art. Hamon held his hand over his mouth in an effort to not vomit. The smell alone was almost enough to do him in. The sight…he didn't even know a sight as sickening as this was possible.

He held his torch above the corpses and overpowered his gagging in order to analyze them. Men, women, children, even some corpses appeared to be infants. No one was spared from this massacre. Among them was a corpse resting on its side to the right of the pile.

Among it…was a corpse he recognized…

Chapter 8

Loss

Lenard stood outside of the entrance of the cave and remained there with Quinton and Picc. No light whatsoever surrounded them. They were left in complete and utter darkness. Quinton's breathing was panicked as he was not experienced in keeping calm in the dark. Lenard left his hand placed on his shoulder for comfort. Picc needed no such comfort.

In reality, his breathing was almost as relaxed, if not even more relaxed, than his own. He questioned how an *Appearer* could have so much experience with *The Forest.*

A slight shimmer of light appeared deep within the cave. The three of them glared at the approaching, orange light. Next to the flame was Hamon. As he grew closer Lenard was able to take further note of his face.

His eyes were lifeless. Like his soul had been sucked from his body. His mouth rested slightly open and he did not glance at any of them, but kept his eyes fixated on the floor beneath him.

Lenard experienced a sickening feeling of dread in his chest. Hamon passed the entrance of the cave and halted next to Lenard and Quinton.

He turned his head toward Hamon, "Did you find her?"

Hamon placed his hand on Lenard to support himself. "...yes...let's go home..."

His eyes grew teary as he scrunched them. He nodded slightly. Hamon walked past him. Quinton and Picc followed him. Lenard stood still behind the group for a brief moment before following them.

Hamon led the way back to the camp with the guidance of the compass. As they traveled, none of them spoke. A terrible silence put a dreadful pressure on the men.

Picc interrupted the silence, "I'm sorry...I never meant for something like this to happen."

Hamon raised his palm to interrupt Picc, "I was supposed to be responsible for her. I was the one who was supposed to look after her. The blame is on me."

"What did you see down there? Other than Kaylee?" Picc asked.

He placed his fingers on the stem of his nose, "You don't want to know."

Picc arched an eyebrow, "Was the monster down there? Any sign of it at least."

"Nothing, the cave is probably just its feeding ground," Hamon said.

Picc sighed, "Right...Do you think the monster will attack us?"

"Probably not, I think it wanted something to eat...now, could we please stop talking about this." Picc nodded. It was going so well, five days in a row with no trouble.

Then, they decide to venture to one more campsite, and it all goes to shit. What were the chances of that? Why didn't they decide to go back when they had plenty of materials?

"Who's going to tell Klyde?" Lenard spoke.

"I will," Hamon placed his hand on his chest. "I was the one who told Klyde to leave Kaylee's safety. Like I said, I'm responsible for her."

"Why don't I tell him with you," Lenard offered.

"No…this is my responsibility alone. You were wiser than me, and yet I didn't listen," Hamon said.

"That's not true…yo…you aren't the only person here at fault. I encouraged her to come too. I was the one who gave you the idea in the first place," Quinton said.

"Yes…yes I am. I was the one who made the final decision to bring her with. Now that's enough. No more discussing who is and isn't at fault, understand." Hamon glanced back and Lenard and Quinton, who both nodded.

No one spoke a word for the rest of the trip. They all soaked in this new reality at their own pace. Hamon could hear some of them let out some whimpers and tears.

When they finally arrived back at the campsite, the main group huddled at the edge of the camp. Klyde and Amber positioned themselves in the front of the group. Hamon knew. However, they did not find Kaylee anywhere.

When they grew closer, Klyde walked past the edge of the camp to approach them.

"Hey…where's Kaylee?" He asked with a quiver.

Hamon forced himself to look Klyde in the eyes, "We…I…she…didn't make it," was all he could muster. Klyde's eyes widened.

"What do you mean?...Where's my daughter Hamon?" He scrunched his eyes as a tear rolled down his cheek. Klyde's shoulders slumped as he re-focused his gaze off Hamon and into the distance.

"I'm sorry…I'm so sorry…" Klyde turned around and walked back toward the main group. His eyes remained gaped the entire time and stood in front of Amber, who looked at him in dread. He placed his hand on her arm and began to cry.

Amber did as well. Their cries turned to sobs. They all began to share tears. The venturers too. All but Picc, who Hamon saw, wear a sorrowful gaze.

Outside was Hamon, who was crouched at the main campfire and stoked the flames. Much of the group had gone back into their tents in order to rest. Across from him at the same fire was Picc, resting at the same spot he was before they left for the expedition.

Both of them ignored the other's presence as they gazed into the fire. Once Hamon was done stoking the flame, he sat himself on the ground. Mark exited from one of the tents near the fire then walked toward Hamon and stood over him.

"Hey…I know you're not going to want to hear this but…I'm sorry. I should have gone with," Mark said.

Hamon sighed, "Don't blame yourself. Don't blame anyone but me."

Mark clenched his fist and gritted his teeth, "But if I were there, maybe the situation could have been different. Maybe it could have been better."

"It could also have been worse." Kaylee was the reason that monster did not fool them. If Mark were there instead, it could have gone *much* worse. "Besides, if you were there the same thing might have happened to you."

"Maybe it should have," He scoffed. Hamon gazed up at him and clenched onto his wrist.

"Don't," he swallowed hard. "Don't say that. Understand?" Mark gave a nod. "Now go rest, you need it." Mark walked back to his tent.

"You don't have to carry all of the blame, you know. To be completely honest you are probably the least responsible person, other than Lenard," Picc claimed.

"It's not about who said what. I was the one who had the final call. I was the one who took responsibility for her. It's my fault," Hamon said.

"Hmph, you…you're nothing like the leaders I've ever seen before. Most leaders I've seen are cold and harsh. They don't let the deaths of their members get to them. In a way, you could argue it's the only way to survive here. But you seem to think differently, and you prove it too. I mean, your group is one of the largest I've seen."

"I know full well how harsh leaders could be. I was in two groups before this one. The first one, our leader, his name was Dan. He'd only take in female venturers, in exchange they had to…procreate with him in order to receive his protection.

He would take his children and raise them to be his loyal venturers. He was my father. He made me begin venturing when I was only twelve years old. I don't know what happened to him…if he's dead or alive, I ran away.

After him, I came across my second group. The leader there was Alex. Then, A monster attacked our village when we were sleeping and killed Alex, along with most of our members. When we ran, we came across Klyde's group. At that time, it was him, Amber…Kaylee, Jean, Alice and Quinton.

Back then Klyde was the leader of the group. He showed me that there was such a thing as a kind leader. He's a great man, a great friend…a great father."

"Sounds like you hold great admiration for him." Hamon nodded.

He then turned to face Picc, "Did you have anyone you held admiration for?"

"My blind friend I told you about. I admired his skill. It would be great if he survived, having him on an expedition, we might find that musket much sooner," Picc said.

"What do you mean, find? You're not still planning on another expedition, are you?" Hamon asked.

Picc shrugged, "Well, of course I am. Like I said, one attempt is not enough. It'll take several, if not even dozens of expeditions before we find it."

"We are not going on another expedition to find that musket. We…already lost enough," Hamon claimed.

"And I am sorry for that but think of what she would have wanted. She wouldn't want us moping around, she would want us to continue the search," Picc claimed. Hamon glared at him. "Not just her, but think of the other members, how they want to find that musket as well. If you really want to be a good leader then you should consider their wants as well."

"Shut the hell up," Hamon stood up. Without looking Picc in the eye once, he shook his head from side to side and walked away. He stopped at the edge of the camp at the bonfire and rested himself back on the ground, alone this time.

At the edge of the campsite a little ways away from him was Lenard. He gazed off into the abyss while leaning against a tree with his arms crossed.

He stared at him for a fleeting moment. As he did, Lenard turned away from the abyss and walked toward the bonfire to join Hamon.

"I saw you walking away from Picc. I guess you guys had a bit of a blowout." Hamon nodded.

Lenard scoffed, "Don't listen to that guy, he for sure has a screw loose."

"I know…but he makes good points," Hamon sighed.

"He doesn't make good shit. I don't care whether or not you want to blame yourself for…what happened. But ever since he got here things have been going to shit," Lenard raged.

Hamon shook his head, "That's not all true. Because of that grand expedition and our haul of food and water, we won't be running low on those for a long time."

"Who cares about that…it doesn't matter if…if we're…whatever. Regardless, I don't like him, I don't trust him," Lenard said.

"You trust me though, don't you?" Hamon asked.

"...With my life…" Lenard whispered.

"Then trust me when I say…it's my fault," Hamon uttered.

"You trust me, right," Lenard gestured toward himself. Hamon nodded. "Then trust me when I say that guys a lying sack of shit."

"Is it…those dreams you claim to be having?" Hamon asked.

Lenard sneered, "...I'm telling you…there's something not right about it. I've had dreams…even back when I was alone. None were like this…none were this vivid or felt this real," he spun his hand around in a circle.

"Besides, I somehow knew what glasses were. After that first dream, it was like what glasses are was slipped into my memory. Like I somehow always knew what they were," he claimed.

"What are glasses?" Hamon asked while raising an eyebrow.

"There are like…little handles that hold pieces of glass in front of your eyes," he circled his hands and placed them around his eyes.

"And why would someone need that?" Hamon questioned with a snicker.

"I don't know…but I knew what they were, somehow. Even though I had no prior knowledge of them. I asked Picc, and he said they were something from the real world. Meaning it doesn't exist here," Lenard said.

"And have you had any more of these…dreams?" Hamon asked.

Lenard exhaled, "...No…They only happened twice. I tried getting some sleep earlier to see if it would happen, but nothing."

"Okay…so…let's say that these dreams are real, that you really are seeing into Picc's old memories. For what reason would that be helpful? How would that help us in our current situation?" Hamon shrugged his left arm.

"I'm…not sure. I feel…that…if we get back out there…maybe I will find out," Lenard muttered.

"You…" Hamon raised his index finger at him. "Want to go back out there?"

"I know…I know I sound crazy right now…but you have to trust me," Lenard bobbed his palms.

"No, you have to trust me," Hamon pointed his thumb to his chest, "Whatever is happening to you right now, it's not like you," Hamon claimed.

"Well, maybe I don't want to be like me right now," Lenard gestured his arms wide. "Maybe even the cynical asshole gets tired of being a cynical asshole from time to time."

Hamon stood up to face Lenard and towered over him in superior height. "Right now, what we need to focus on is Kaylee…and how we're going to honor her. We don't have time to speculate…whatever this is right now."

Lenard scoffed, "You think I haven't been thinking about Kaylee…I'm hurt just as much as you are. A good kid like her didn't deserve what happened to her…she was the last person who deserved that-"

"Then why don't you act like it?" Hamon swung his hand in his direction. "Seriously, you of all people…you sulk and complain whenever someone gets a scratch on an expedition-"

"Well I'm tired of that…I'm tired of not doing anything. I'm tired of thinking that everything is hopeless," he raged.

"Why are you talking to me like something crazy is happening!" Hamon said.

"Something crazy is happening! I'm the only one who's acting like there isn't! We were attacked by a monster no one has seen before. And we're acting like that's no big deal. Like we've run into something like that every couple of days!" Lenard screamed.

"Alright, alright..." He sighed. "We'll talk about this later...we shouldn't fight...not at a time like this."

"Right...sorry I got a little heated. I'm just...trying to think of what Kaylee would do in this situation." Lenard walked over and kneeled down next to Hamon. The both of them stared at the fire for a brief moment. "She was a good kid...she should have been living a good life, sitting here listening to her parents lecture her or something."

"I know...but we still have people we need to look after. They're all torn up about as much as we are. We have to focus on them right now," Hamon said.

"I understand, I'll do that with you. But we need to get back out there," Lenard claimed.

"If you think things are crazy right now...then why are you so eager about *The Forest* all of the sudden," Hamon claimed.

Lenard clenched his fist, "Because...I have a feeling there's something out there. Something that could help. But also something about Picc. Maybe it's something about how he has all these memories from the other world. I don't know...but I want to find out." Hamon nodded.

"Right...why not for now...you go get some rest." Lenard nodded as he stood up and left out of sight into one of the tents.

Hamon sat alone.

The edge fire crackled in front of him. He gazed into the fire as countless thoughts loomed in an endless loop in his head. Then, chatter erupted from afar. It was too far for him to hear anything.

He thought to check it out himself, but he didn't, he did not feel like it. He did not feel like doing anything at all, except give it up.

Jean approached from his side, "Hamon!" She called.

He glanced up and met her gaze, "what is it?" He asked in a pathetic tone.

"Klyde is calling us to the center, he says that Picc has an idea," Jean said. Hamon felt a sense of uneasiness.

Chapter 9

Laborers

Klyde gathered all of the group members in a circle at the center of the campsite, as to Picc's request. All of them sat side by side and whispered to each other.

On one side of the fire, Amber stood next to Klyde. He leaned in toward him, "Hey, what's this all about?"

"I'm not too sure about it myself. I think Picc has some news to share with us." Amber stared at him.

Next to Klyde on the other side of Amber, Picc stepped forward. He placed his foot atop one of the rocks surrounding the campfire, "Thank you all for gathering here for me. I have some information that I wish to share with you. It's regarding a second attempt at a grand expedition."

"We've talked about this, a second grand expedition isn't happening," Hamon announced.

"Not without a change in plans that is." Picc held up the piece of paper and faced it toward the group. They squinted to see what markings lied on the paper. "Here in my hands are blueprints to a device that we'll make venturing significantly safer for all of us. It's the blueprints to a device called a flashlight."

"If a device like that really exists then why are you only mentioning it now?" Mark asked.

"It was not possible to craft before. But now...because of the bow that was brought back by......because of the bow, we now have string. This string will allow us to make a sort of generator that will power this flashlight," Picc said.

Hamon scoffed, "It doesn't matter. I said before that a second expedition isn't happening." The group remained quiet. Whereas before some would protest, none did.

Klyde cleared his throat, "I think we should try again." Hamon glanced at him in shock. "That's what Kaylee would want. She wouldn't want me...nor anyone here to mope around because of her."

Amber glared an angry look at him, "You can't be serious? After what we lost?"

"And we'll only lose more if we stand around doing nothing," Klyde said back. Amber shook her head.

"If we are to do this. We'll need help from everyone. We may even have to go on a few side expeditions in order to collect materials for this. I'll work with all of you to assign each of you a task," Picc claimed.

"H-Hold on...You aren't the boss here, you can't go ordering our people around," Hamon protested.

"I'm aware, for those who wish to not participate, you are welcome to. I'm not going to attempt to convince anyone this time. I will, however, attempt to persuade you," Picc claimed.

"None of us are helping you with anything. We are not going on another expedition," Hamon gestured his hands to the group.

"Your friend here seems to disagree," Picc waved toward Klyde.

Hamon sneered, "It…It doesn't matter what he says, I'm telling you, right now, we are not going on another grand expedition."

"It doesn't matter what he says?" Quinton scoffed. "I think it matters a lot what he has to say. He is our leader. I think what he has to say matters most."

"You don't have to argue for me. If Hamon wants to ignore what I have to say then that's how it is," Klyde shrugged.

"I'm not trying to ignore you, I'm trying to keep this group safe." Hamon gazed over each member of the group. Amber nodded, Mark, and Alice bowed down their heads. Quinton and Jarold shook their heads.

Jean shrugged, "Sorry. But I think Picc is right. Even if we don't go on another grad expedition, I don't see why we still can't make this flashlight thing."

"Hmph," then, he glanced over to Lenard. "Come on man, back me up here." Lenard looked back at him. He wore a face of guilt.

"I…I'm sorry Hamon, but for once, I'm finding myself siding with Picc." Hamon scoffed, then crossed his arms.

"It appears you need some time to discuss this over with your group. I'll start working on who will do what, in the meantime, I'll let you have your discussion." Picc stepped away from the fire and walked off into the distance. Some of the members went to follow him. Other members went back to whatever they were doing.

Lenard and Hamon shared eye contact one last time. Then Lenard bowed his head shamefully as he walked away. Hamon refocused his gaze on Klyde, who he began approaching along with Amber. The two of them halted at Klyde's feet.

"Klyde, what the hell do you think you're doing?!" Hamon questioned.

He turned to him, "I'm doing what I think is best. What I think will be best for this camp."

"What's best for this camp is not whatever the hell that guy thinks it is. He's messing with us, trying to turn us against each other," Hamon claimed.

Klyde arched an eyebrow, "He's trying to turn us against each other by helping us? Hamon, you're letting your pride get the best of you here."

"No, I'm not. Only an hour ago I told him how I admire you as a leader, then all the sudden he wants you on his side?" He questioned.

Klyde placed his hand on his chest, "I want to be on his side. I was the one that came to him and asked him if he was going to try again for another expedition."

"Why?" Amber looked at him with an expression filled with hurt. "After what we lost? You're going to try to put more of our people through that? Don't you feel anything?"

Klyde clenched his eyes, "Of course I do. That's why I want to do this."

"And get more of our family killed?" Amber hovered her arm across the campsite.

"So they won't! You know how many groups I've gone through. Seven! Seven times I have had to watch people I considered family die! Each and every time it was the same. …Kaylee…" he sighed, "Kaylee had the spirit to change things, to make things different. If I have to watch a family die for an eighth time, I'm going to make sure it's at least different." He glanced away and walked off without saying another word.

Amber began to sniffle, then too walked off into one of the tents. Hamon watched as Klyde approached Picc and began discussing something with him. His expression morphed from irritated to bitter. Picc was untrustworthy, he knew it, he just didn't know how to prove it. He turned away and followed Amber into her tent. He opened up the zipper to find her crying, quickly wiping the tears away.

"You don't need to comfort me, I can handle myself." She waved her hand in a gesture shewing him away.

"You've always been there to comfort me when I came home with injuries, now you aren't going to let me do the same with you?" She smiled as she rolled her eyes. He sat himself down a couple feet across from her.

"I appreciate it, really. But I promise I'll be fine…it's just…a bad time right now." She wiped a tear from her eye.

"I know, we don't have to talk about that…we can talk about something else." Hamon proposed.

"What else is there to talk about?" She asked.

"I don't know…" he sighed.

She glanced toward the wall of the tent, "What's going on with Lenard? It's not like him to want to go out on expeditions."

"I don't know about him either," he contemplated telling Amber about the dreams Lenard was having.

"So neither of us have any idea what's going on. Neat." Amber let out a deep sigh as she leaned back. She was right.

He suspected that Lenard may be right about Picc planning something, but there was no way he could prove that. He felt as if the group was being torn away from him.

"So…are we going to talk or are you just going to stare off into the distance the entire time," Amber laughed.

He snapped out of his train of thought. "Sorry," he whispered. Amber giggled. "I know Lenard wants to go on this expedition, but I can say at the very least he's still on our side."

She raised an eyebrow, "So we're taking sides now?"

"I know…I don't like the idea of it either. But I can't help but think Picc is an enemy," he glared.

"Then why don't you go out there and stop him." She gestured toward the zipper of the tent.

"I tried that, you tried that. We both saw how that went," he said.

"I don't mean by talking things out. I mean why don't you go out there and slice his head open with your ax, problem solved." Hamon squinted at her. "I'm messing with you. But I wouldn't be entirely opposed to the idea."

"It's not like you at all to want somebody dead," Hamon said.

She shrugged, "What can I say, to me he's pretty much the sole reason my daughter's gone. I don't give a rat's ass what happens to him."

"I told you already, what…happened to Kaylee is on me," Hamon placed his hand on his chest.

"Oh quit it with that bullshit," she waved her hand at him. "You were the only one other than Lenard trying to stop her from going."

"I told Klyde that Kaylee was my responsibility," Hamon claimed.

"And you protected her the best you could. But you're not invincible," she said.

Hamon slightly nodded then peered off into the distance. Amber did the same, as she did, tears began to well her eyes.

She sniffled, "You know…I remember when she was a little girl, she would get all snuggly under her covers. I would come and cuddle her as I told her all those memories of the other world I had. About the skies…the fields…the snow," she whipped another tear from her eye.

"The look of wonder she had. It felt like for once, I was truly seeing a miracle come true in this world. Before…I would give anything to see her smile and have a sparkle in her eyes like that. If…If I knew it would lead to this…I would take it all back. I was being selfish…wanting to see that miracle. I'm a monster for that," she said.

"Giving her something to be happy about and believe in doesn't make you a monster," Hamon gave her a smile.

Amber smiled back, then whipped away her tears again. "Thank you…I appreciate you coming to talk with me. But…I think I should get some rest." Hamon nodded as he stood upward.

"We'll talk again sometime, I promise you that," Hamon said. He could hear her giggle, along with the shuffling of the tent floor as he exited the tent. He glanced back at the tent, then refocused his gaze across the campsite.

Many of the group members were trouting around. He noticed they were moving as per Picc's instructions. He was still at the center of the camp, standing atop a rock and pointed in different directions.

Klyde was among them. He stood right next to Picc. He analyzed the members as they moved about. He rarely took his sight off of them.

Some of the members grabbed water flasks from the chests scattered around the camp. Others were huddled together in a small group. Hamon approached Picc.

He glanced upward at him and analyzed his smug smile and overarching gaze. "What the hell is going on?"

Picc looked downward and met Hamon's sight. "We're moving ahead with the plan, is that not obvious?"

"I thought you said you would give us time to discuss it as a group," Hamon claimed.

"I have. Most of the members talked with each other and came to the conclusion that they will help me," Picc shrugged.

"Why wasn't I a part of this?" Hamon pointed toward his chest.

"You are a part of this. You can still voice your displeasure with our plan. But at the end of the day the other members made up their minds," Picc smiled.

"You know that's not what I mean," Hamon glared.

Picc snickered, "Oh, I know what you mean. You mean why weren't you a part of the conversation so you could demand that everyone listen to you."

"Wha…no, what the group does affects me. If they go along with your plan then I have to as well," Hamon claimed.

"Then get with the crowd," Picc gestured his arms out wide.

Hamon raised his eyebrows, "Wha-What?" Picc stepped down from the rock.

"It's a metaphor. It means either help us…or get out of our way." He patted Hamon's shoulder as he walked away. Hamon glanced toward him, before he turned back around and met Klyde's gaze. He did not speak to him but glared. After a brief moment, Klyde began to follow Picc, walking right past Hamon.

"Hold on," Hamon demanded. Picc and Klyde halted.

"What is it?" Picc asked.

Hamon sighed, "Tell me what to do."

Picc grinned as he reapproached Hamon. "I'm glad to hear you're on our side."

"Yeah…don't make me regret it. Give me a rundown of what we're doing," Hamon said.

"Right, the first thing on the chopping black right now is we need to make a rudimentary watermill," Picc said.

Hamon raised his brow, "And what's that?"

"A mill that gets pushed in a constant motion by flowing water. In the other world, they would make these by using rivers. We don't have that here, so we'll need to make our own makeshift river. The best thing you could do for me is chop down some trees," he gestured toward the trees that surrounded them.

Hamon furrowed his brow, "Ex-excuse me?"

"Use your hatchet to chop down a tree, we're going to need its wood. Is that a problem?" Picc asked while he had his hands on his hips.

"Knocking down the trees will remove our cover. Monsters will be able to spot us more easily," Hamon gestured toward the trees.

"We'll use the wood from the trees to build more campfires. That will help us expand. We'll need that extra space for what we're doing. I'll explain everything else to you later," Picc waved Hamon off.

"If you say so." He retrieved his hatchet left next to Maner's tent, then wandered off to the edge of the camp and halted at a tree. He gulped as he placed his other hand further down the handle and raised the hatchet to his side.

He spread out his feet, then took a mighty swing at the tree. The sound of the hatchet clashing with the wood echoed across the camp. The hatchet team aimed lodged between the oak wood of the tree. Hamon thrusted backward in an attempt to pull the hatchet out from the wood, but failed, then tried again, succeeding this time.

He spread his feet out wide once more, then took another swing at the tree. Splinters of wood burst out from the impact. The loose branches and forest green leaves gracefully fell to the ground as the tree shook.

Then he took another swing. The cut was deep enough that the inner wood of the tree began to crackle. A couple more swings and the cut was halfway through the tree, he then sensed that another swing or two would knock the tree down. He turned back to look for anyone in his area.

The rest of the group was off near the fires, quite a distance from Hamon and now noticed the true distance between him and everyone else. He turned his head back toward the tree.

He looked beyond it out into the void where the orange light from the flame ended. He shook his head as he repositioned himself for another swing. The swing embedded deep into the tree.

The cracking of wood became louder and louder as the tree began to lean. The last bit of wood holding the tree onto its stump snapped. It fell to its side and collided with the branches of the tree next to it before crashing onto the ground. The loud thud caught the rest of the group's attention for a brief moment in time.

Hamon gazed at the stump that now littered the ground, then glanced once more out into the void before hurrying off back to Picc and Klyde.

"Alright, the tree's chopped down, now where do you want me to bring it?" Hamon asked.

Picc glanced at Hamon from the paper his eyes were buried in, he then looked at the chopped tree behind him. "Leave it there for now. We'll move it when it's time. As of right now, the next step is something we're all going to have to work together on."

"And what is that?" Hamon questioned.

Picc flipped the paper in his hands to face Hamon. "We need to build a furnace. In terms of materials, this is actually the easiest thing to make. It's putting it together that will be the hard part."

Hamon raised his index finger to the paper, "Could you explain to me what a…furnace is."

"It's nothing complicated, just a wall of stone surrounding a fire to make it hotter," Picc spun his hand.

"What's a hotter fire going to do for us? Make a stronger lantern?" Hamon asked.

"Nope," Picc waved his finger, "making this furnace is really just the first step. We're going to need it in order to smelt down metal."

"We've burned metals in the fire before, left them for hours even, nothing happened. I doubt that's going to work," Hamon claimed.

Picc shook his head with a confident smile. "That's where you're wrong. When the fire is out in the open, much of its heat escapes. If we surround it with a wall of stone, that heat will remain trapped. Not to mention there are other methods we can use to make it even hotter."

"So this wall of stone will make the fire hot enough to smelt metal? If that's the case, isn't this musket made from wood and iron, could we not make our own?" Hamon bent his arms outward.

"There are two problems with that," Picc held his hand in the air with two fingers pointing out. "One, the design of the musket is too complex for any of us to smelt, we would need someone with years of experience.

Two, even if we did make it through trial and error, we don't know how it works. It could randomly malfunction, or not work at all. That could get us killed in an expedition."

"Alright…then where do we get started for this furnace thing?" Klyde stepped forward and pointed toward a smaller gathering of four members huddled together.

"We're having some of the group members putting together the stone bricks right now." Hamon nodded.

"Once they're finished with that, we'll begin working on the furnace." Picc cleared his throat, "You may even need to cut down some more trees, I'm not sure if one log will be enough, but we'll see."

"What do we do in the meantime?" Hamon asked.

"We wait, you can rest if you would like, I still need to work on the blueprints some more," Picc said.

Hamon turned to Klyde, "What about you, Klyde?"

"I have to keep watch over the camp, you're welcome to join me in that exhilarating job," he said half smiling.

"I'll pass on that," He waved his hand at him.

Picc walked, "I'll be working on the blueprints over by the center, I'll be there if you need me."

Klyde and Hamon watched as Picc walked far enough away to leave him out of earshot of the two of them.

Klyde turned to Hamon, fixating his gaze to him. "Hey…I appreciate you helping us. We'll be able to get this done a lot faster with your help."

Hamon met his eyesight. "Yeah, no problem…but uhh…are you going to talk to Amber about this sometime soon? She's still upset with you."

Klyde turned his gaze back to the camp. "I don't blame her. But I don't blame myself either. I understand why to her it seems like I'm pretending like nothing happened. It's just…I couldn't bear to stand another goddamn second not doing anything," he let out a deep sigh.

"Isn't that just ignoring it? Maybe you should take the time to sit down and process it," Hamon proposed.

Klyde softly nodded. “Maybe…but either way, I don’t care. That’s not what I am going to do.” Hamon burrowed his lips and kept his eyes focused on Klyde.

“Well, don’t let that ruin what you two have going on. Both of you are better than that.” Hamon patted Klyde’s shoulder.

“I’m going to go rest now…take it easy, will you?” Hamon smiled at him. Klyde kept his gaze focused on the camp. His smile faded as his eyes fell lower. He walked to one of the tents and opened the zipper, then took one last look at Klyde. He sighed, then entered the tent.

Chapter 10

Leader

Lenard stood at the edge of the camp. The fire's warm light barley graced him. The clacking and speaking of the members of the camp echoed to the edge of the camp. He leaned against a tree, his arms wrapped around each other. His head was pointed toward the brown dirt in front of him. His eyes felt like blankets, like just a blink would cause him to pass out.

A loud clunk from the campsite jolted him awake. He darted his eyes toward the center of the camp. In the center he saw Picc and Klyde. They were not discussing anything but stood side by side. He wondered when they managed to become such good friends.

He pushed himself forward and stood upright, then walked back to the center of the camp. The production that went on within became visible to him, along with the loud noises of sloshing, footsteps and talking. Lines of stone rectangles were being put together, where Hamon stood at the end. He received the stone from Jarold. The lines of stone were located a dozen feet from the main campfire. In that same location, regular stone rocks were lined in a circle.

Klyde stood firm, his hands connected behind his back. He would on occasion, reach one of his hands out to point at the ground, where Hamon would then place a stone that he had received. Their discussion became audible to Lenard as he came closer. He could hear Klyde giving Hamon instructions. When he came close enough, Klyde and Picc took notice of him.

Klyde gave him a welcoming nod, then turned his gaze back to Hamon, who then also noticed Lenard. He stood up from his leaning position to meet Lenard's gaze.

"So…you're helping them now," Lenard said.

Hamon smirked, "Better than doing nothing."

Lenard snickered, "I doubt that. Anything looks better than this."

Picc wore a creepy smile as he approached Lenard, "You're just in time. I could use your help. We are going to need some venturers to gather certain materials."

He raised his arms and pushed them against the air. "Woah there…I never said I would be helping you with anything."

Picc furrowed his brow, "I thought you were one of the people who was for the flashlight idea."

"I'm for going on another expedition. I don't give a damn about this flashlight thing," he said.

Picc's unsettling smile returned. "Well then, this job is just for you. You are going to be doing exactly that. You'll be taking Jean and Alice with you. Those two volunteered as well."

Lenard squirted his eyes and sharpened his eyebrows. "I meant another grand expedition. Besides, we don't go on expeditions without either Klyde or Hamon. We need a team leader with us."

Hamon stepped over the lines of stone, then halted a couple feet away from Lenard as he placed his hands on his hips. “I think you could handle an expedition on your own.”

Lenard re-focused his sharpened gaze on Hamon. “I’m glad you have confidence in me. But in all seriousness, that’s not going to happen.”

“I mean it!” Hamon gestured toward him. “Even before we met Picc, making you an expedition leader was something I had been considering. You can handle an expedition a lot better than you think you can.”

Lenard shook his head. “No…I can’t.” He glanced at Picc, then placed his hand on Hamon’s shoulder and led him a couple feet away. He leaned toward him, “You can’t expect me to go on an expedition by myself. What if…I…I can’t handle it.”

“You’ll do just fine, I know you will,” Hamon waved his hand at him. “You’re not that kid lost in the woods on his own anymore. You have people. You have sense. I know, you know that. That’s why it hasn’t happened in a long time.”

Lenard placed his hand on his forehead and slid it up to his hair, “Sure…maybe I have some sense now, but I don’t know how to lead them,” he gestured toward the spread out ventures.

“Give it a try, based on what Picc has told me this expedition will be a small one, only a couple of hours. If something goes wrong, or you still don’t feel like you’re ready, then we’ll wait,” Hamon said.

Lenard sighed, “Fine…” he nodded as he began to leave Lenard’s grip. Lenard pulled him back. “I have one more thing to ask you. Why the hell are you helping Picc? Truly.”

Hamon closed his eyes and relaxed his expression. “Because…If Picc really is our enemy, then I cannot afford to be in the dark about what he’s doing. I have to be vigilant and know what he’s up to. Amber had a metaphor for that…keep your friends close and your enemies closer.”

Lenard smirked, “I should have known…you are the type of guy to think ahead like that.” He released Hamon from his grip and then reapproached Picc. “Alright…you win. You mentioned there were certain materials you wanted me to collect, give me a list.”

Picc’s smile widened as he reached into his coat pocket and pulled out a piece of folded paper. Lenard reached out his hand and placed his palm on the piece of paper, then unfolded it. Listed on the paper was 240 grams of iron, 815 grams of copper, 1.1 kilograms of rubber, 60ft of rope, 100 grams of glass.

Picc overlapped his finger on the paper, “I made sure to make it detailed.”

Lenard smirked, “Yeah…obnoxiously so. I hate to break the bad news to you, but it’s not exactly like we are going to be carrying a scale out there.”

Picc nodded, “I’m aware. You will have to do some eyeballing. The list is only meant to give general estimates of what we may need.”

“Neat,” Leaned said. Picc stepped back to his original position. He pointed to the list of items, “There is one question I have about this. Sixty feet of rope were lucky to even find twenty. The grand expedition we only found fifty feet of rope.”

"I know, I'm not saying you have to get every item listed there, only most of what you can. Getting the rest of that rope will require multiple expeditions," Picc said.

"Right…" He placed the piece of paper into his pocket, then pointed his thumb backwards. "I guess I'll go collect Jean and Alice now." Picc nodded as Lenard turned his back toward them.

He scanned the campsite to find the two of them. They were at the edge bonfire from the left of Picc, Hamon and Klyde. They were huddled around the fire, looking at something.

He recognized them by their signature long, smooth, reddish blonde hair. The color was still easy to notice despite the harsh shadows on their backs generated by the fire light.

The two were next to each other. Jean was on the right, the tell being that her hair is shorter and darker, and also that Alice always wears her hair in a ponytail.

Huddled with them was Quinton and Mark, Mark was next to Alice, Quinton was next to Jean. Their muffled conversation became audible as he came closer. Certain words became understandable and he could hear words like stone, and MREs leave their mouths, although he did not bother to listen to much. He halted right behind Alice and tapped his index finger on the edge of her shoulder. She jumped slightly as she ceased her conversation, then turned to see Lenard.

She placed her hand on her heart, "Jeez, you spooked me." The others had now taken notice of him, directing their gazes to him.

Lenard smirked, "Well try to be more alert next time. Or I might try to actually scare you."

Alice rolled her eyes and shook her head while smiling. He chuckled. "What is it you need?" She asked.

"The preacher wants us to go on an expedition for some materials," Lenard tilted his head toward Picc.

She furrowed her brows. "Are you talking about Picc? *You're* working with him? Man…I would have never guessed that in a million years."

Lenard waved his hand at her, "Yeah, yeah, get over it. I'm tired of hearing that from people."

She smirked as she placed her hand on her hip, "So Picc wants us to venture for materials. Who's going to be our leader?"

He closed his eyes, raised his eyebrows and smiled. "I am." He then raised his forearm and pointed his index finger into his chest.

Alice's eyes widened as she slightly leaned her head forward, "You? Man…you got me doubly surprised."

Lenard smirked, "Yep, I know. Finally happening."

She smiled as she placed her hand on his shoulder. "Good for you, really. Honestly, I thought Quinton would make an expedition leader before you did."

He raised her arms and gently pushed Alice off of him. "Don't get too excited. It's not official, we're just trying it out to see how I do. Besides, Quinton only wishes he were as good of a venturer as me."

"I'm right here you know," Quinton slanted his eyebrows.

"I don't see how that makes it any less true," Lenard smirked. Jean and Alice laughed.

"Damn, get burned," Jean mocked. He smiled as he shook his head and took his gaze off of Lenard, the resumed whatever activity he had been doing.

"So…who ya bringing?" Jean asked.

"You, me and you," Lenard pointed his finger at Alice. Jean's eyes lit up as she smiled. Alice's lips parted as she glanced at Jean before looking back at Lenard. She was biting her lip.

"Jean is coming? But she's only been on a handful of expeditions."

Lenard raised his hand at her. "Don't worry, this is a small expedition. We'll only be out for a couple of hours. It's no less dangerous than a normal expedition."

"On normal expeditions we have Hamon or Klyde leading us. No offense Lenard, but I don't fully trust you as a leader," Alice noted.

Lenard nodded, "I get it. But you'll be coming too, both of us will be keeping an eye on her."

Jean grabbed her sister's arm, "C'mon, it's just a normal expedition. I've gone on those before."

Alice sighed, "As long as I am able to keep an eye on her. So…when do we leave?"

"As soon as we are ready to go. I'm not sure about you guys but I have some things I need to prepare. Jean, you'll be our carrier. Alice, you'll be our lookout. Knowing you two, I'm going to bring the torch, so I'll be the torch-holder," Lenard pointed toward himself.

Alice nodded, "Alright. I guess while you're doing that I'll brush Jean up on some venturing etiquette."

Lenard nodded again as he turned his back toward them, "Meet me at the other edge bonfire when you're ready!"

"Okay!" Alice shouted back. He approached a tent near the center fire. On the left on the entrance was a chest filled with two unlit torches and cloth. He grabbed one of the torches, holding the end opposite of the black, charred cloth, then took the fresh cloth and wrapped it around the charred remains of the previous one.

He wrapped it tight so it wouldn't fall off. Once he finished wrapping it, he walked to the center bonfire, across from Picc, Klyde and Hamon who still worked on lining the stone, then placed his foot on one of the rocks surrounding the fire. He dipped the cloth end of the torch into the fire. He let it sit there until he noticed parts of the white cloth growing darker.

Fire now ignited the cloth end of the torch. He burrowed the plain wood end into the ground and left the torch sticking upright on its own.

He then turned back to another tent next to the other one. Hiking bags littered the tent's sides, and he picked up three of them and grabbed all of them by the straps with his two hands. Carrying them to the center fire and laying them next to the torch.

He opened a chest next to the center fire that contained all of their MREs and water flasks. He took out three of each, then closed the chest and brought the materials back to the hiking bags, where he spread each of the items into the three bags.

He grabbed all of the bags by their right straps and wrapped them around his shoulder. He carefully removed the torch from the ground. He then carried all of the items to the edge bonfire.

As he approached the edge bonfire, Alice and Jean followed him, tagging a bit from behind. Once Lenard was at the fire, he turned and waited for the two of them to reach him.

When they did, he passed each of them a hiking bag. Both of them wrapped the bags around their backs.

He took a deep breath, "Alright, let's lay some ground rules. Since I have the torch, you two can talk, but no shouting. *Nothing* above a normal talking voice, you understand," He pointed his finger at each of them one at a time. Both of them nodded when he did.

He placed one hand on his hip and another reaching in for the piece of paper. "This piece of paper is all the materials Picc wants us to collect. We don't need to get everything. Just most of it." He placed the piece of paper into Alice's fingers.

She unfolded the paper and held the two edges by her thumb. Her eyes shifted down the paper before she nodded, she then turned her hip toward Jean and stretched out her arm in her direction. Jean reached out her hand and grasped onto the slip of paper. She held and read it the same as her sister, before handing it back to Lenard. He placed the slip of paper into his coat pocket.

He cleared his throat, "If you guys come across any of those materials, let me know. We'll grab any MREs or water flasks we come across as well. Everything else, leave it behind. If there's something you find that you think could be useful, let me know." Alice and Jean nodded.

"Let's get a move on then. Follow my lead." He turned his back toward them. They walked away from the edge bonfire and exited the edge of the camp. The light from the bonfire faded as the light of the torch swallowed the area around them. He could hear the shallow footsteps of Alice and Jean following him from behind. A brief moment of silence before he heard the shifting of Jean's clothing as she moved her hip.

"So…." Jean whispered.

"Quiet," Lenard hushed.

"Come on, didn't you bring the torch so we could talk," she said.

"That doesn't mean I want to listen," Lenard smirked.

He heard the swipe of air as Jean waved her arm, "I was just going to ask what we need these materials for anyway."

He turned his neck to side eye her, "Don't know, don't care. All I know is he needs 'em."

Jean furrowed her brow, "You didn't even ask? I shouldn't be surprised," she shrugged.

Lenard re-fixed his gaze in front of him, "And you didn't?"

Jean's arms slapped each side of her hip, "I did! All he would tell me is 'I'll see.' Whatever the hell that means."

"Same with me," Alice sighed.

Lenard raised his forearm and pointed upwards, "One, keep your voices down. Two, if he said that to you two, he probably would have said the same thing to me." He brought his arm back down. Jean softly groaned behind him.

"Hey, I have my own question. Why are you helping Picc?" He glanced back at Alice and stared at her for a brief moment.

"I have my reasons." Alice sneered in response and shook her head. He rolled his eyes as he once again pulled his gaze forward.

"Well, honestly I like what's going on. It's felt like forever since we all worked on something together. It feels uniting," Alice said.

"Yeah, when's the last time we really worked on something together…it had to be…when we first put up the camp together," Jean added. Lenard raised his hand and spread his fingers. Jean and Alice's footsteps stopped. Lenard squinted and leaned his head forward.

"Fire up ahead." He pointed to his left in Jean's general direction.

"I see it," Jean said. In the distance was a small orange dot. The light shifted slightly every so often due to the waving of the flames. Lenard waved his hand to tell Jeans and Alice to follow him. The sound of their footsteps and crackling of fire from the torch swallowed all of the sound.

The orange dot of light became bigger as they reached the campsite. Then, the light of the fire barely began to touch them. The sound of crackling fire and the signature smell of smoke entered their senses. A camp of two tents both ten feet away from the fire on opposite sides.

The tents were of medium size. A chest laid on the visible side of the tent to the left of the group. Lenard halted when he was only two dozen feet away from the fire. Jean and Alice's footsteps silenced as well. Lenard turned toward Alice and Jean who focused their gazes on him.

"I'll search the tents," He focused his gaze on Jean. "Do you know how to do ground search properly?"

Jean raised her forearm and waved her hand at him, "Yes, sir."

Lenard furrowed his brow, then switched his sight to Alice, "Make sure she does it correctly for me." Alice smirked as she nodded as Jean sneered and crossed her arms.

Lenard turned his back toward them and walked to the tent with the brown chest next to it. It was a chest made of oak wood, outlined with rusted iron. The lock had rusted off long ago.

He crouched down in front of it, placing the palm of his hand on the latch of the chest. It was moist in texture, he could feel the small slivers of eroded wood on his fingertips. He pushed the latch upwards and it swung into the tent beside it. He hovered the torch above the chest to bask it in light. Within the chest was a length of rope and a crowbar. He picked out the rope first, grabbing it with his free hand.

It was wrapped into a circle, he guessed it was somewhere around fifteen feet, not a bad find. He tossed the rope to his left side, landing closer to the campfire. He reached his hand back into the chest and grabbed the crowbar by the center of the handle.

Cold metal tinged his hand. He analyzed the crowbar. It too was rusted, but due to the thicker iron, not as much as the chest. He placed it next to him. He stood up and reached behind the chest to its latch, grabbing its edge as he flung it closed.

The slamming of moist wood and metal boomed. He witnessed Jean and Alice glance up at him for a moment in the corner of his eye.

He placed his free hand on the bottom of the torch handle as he slid his other hand up, then he burrowed the torch into the ground deep enough to allow it to stand on its own and turned his hip back toward the crowbar lying on the ground.

He picked it up with two hands this time, one in the middle and one toward the swindle on the bottom, then positioned the crowbar to latch it to the screw in the top right corner of the chest.

With one quick motion, the screw shot off onto the ground as the metal casing loosened slightly. He relodged the crowbar into the middle right screw and shot it off the same as the other and repeated this process with all of the six screws that lined the front-right corner of the chest.

The metal casing fell onto the ground, bits of rust spurted off into a dust cloud as the casing landed. Lenard grabbed it and lined it behind him. He removed all of the other screws lining the chest until all of the metal casings all de-attached.

The metal casings were all lined together in a neat row. Lenard knelt down on one knee facing the casings. The same direction facing away from the camp into *The Forest.*

He removed his bag and placed it next to him, opening the zipper wide enough to create a sizable gap, then used his two hands to scoop all of the metal casings.

He released the metal casings as they fell firmly into his bag as he angled it to not puncture the MREs that also resided within. He closed the zipper of the bag, then re-wrapped it around his back, then swung the lace around his arm.

The metal casings made a muffled clunk. He turned back to face Jean and Alice and expected to find them still searching the ground, only to find no one there.

A swift spike of panic entered his heart. He stood up on his toes to look above the tent on the other side, blocking the only part of the camp from his view. No one stood there.

His panic grew and he raced over to where he last saw the two of them. His head turned one way, then another, then another. Each view yielded no sight of the sisters. Where had they gone? They were just in his sight. He swore he had just heard their voices.

He used his hands to cup the area around his mouth, "Alice! Jean!" His voice echoed, nothing returned. That's when he heard a noise that sent a shiver down his spine and caused his breathing to quiver.

Breathing from above.

Chapter 11

Wandering Wonders

Lenard's eyes opened and let him view a slit of fuzziness. There was a view of an orange glinted tree trunks, a black void beyond it. His vision cleared, the ridges and crevices of the trunks became visible.

Behind him, there were muffled voices. The smell of cooked MREs entered his senses.

He glanced down toward his lap, where he held an MRE in his right. His left hand hovered over the MRE, with a spoon in that hand. He felt the texture of a large stone applied to his back. The sharp but curvy crevices were the tell.

His legs spread outward. Orange light alluded from behind his resting place. The harsh shadow made it impossible to see the end of the spoon resting in the MRE. He released the spoon from his fingertips and placed his hand on his forehead. He rubbed the surface of it, hoping to clear the uneasiness he felt. His dizziness settled and breathed in, then breathed out.

His stomach growled and he placed his hand on it, then groaned as he re-grasped the spoon. Brown broth, with tiny slivers of chicken, littered the end of it. A scent of fresh chicken blessed his nostrils. He opened his mouth as he placed the spoon within, closed his mouth and slid the spoon out.

All of the broth left touching his tongue. A sweet flavor of marinated chicken and peppers enchanted his taste buds. He chewed on the slivers of chicken until they were mush, then swallowed it in magnificent glory. He did not think the taste of MREs could be this sweet. It reminded him of his old days, on his own, when food was a scarcity.

The muffled talking that still persisted behind him became audible. He recognized the voice of Marvin, as well as the captain and black-haired man. There was also new voices, one's he felt he recognized, but could not draw up any memory of. That's when he realized he was in another one of the dream sequences.

He could not remember what happened before this point. All he knew was that he was doing something with Jean and Alice. He could not remember what, or where that left off. He scooped up what little remained in his MRE and placed all of the goods into his mouth.

He set the now empty MRE to his right, then shifted his left arm behind him and shifted his left hand on the rock to lift himself off of the ground.

He balanced himself on his two legs, then looked behind him. There, a camp littered with over a dozen tents, four fires and somewhere around twenty people wondering about. They were either at the fires, resting at trees, or he could see their silhouette peeking through the fabric of the tents.

There were four people at the fire he was closest to, the one casting the orange light on him. Marvin, the black-haired man and the captain, along with someone he recognized but did not know the name of.

He was timid, no larger than one-hundred and thirty pounds. His hair was short, curly and bright brown. He was gazing toward the ground, a nervous expression on his face. His hands were coddled together, and his feet were tapping the ground. Lenard removed his gaze from him to analyze the other three.

To his left, Marvin was standing above the fire, stoking it with a metal rod. To the right, the captain sat on a horizontal oak log, his arms were crossed, staring directly into the fire. The black-haired man sat on the ground resting his back against the same log the captain sat on.

Lenard stepped closer to the fire, Marvin heard his step and looked toward his direction. "Hey, are you looking for some more food?"

The mention of food made Lenard's stomach twitch, "Uhh…nah, that's fine."

Marvin re-focused his gaze into the fire, "Why don't you come have a seat with us then? I'm sure there's lots you want to discuss with us."

Lenard smirked, "I guess I do." He walked over to the left with Marvin and took a seat at another horizontal log on the opposite side of the fire. Marvin's body now covered his view of the black-haired man.

The wave of flames somewhat obscured the captain as well. Marvin retrieved the stoker out of the fire, placed two hands on it, then drove it into the ground. He released it, and it now stood on its own. Marvin took a few short steps toward Lenard, then turned around and bent his knees where he placed his rear on the log. The curly-haired man was now to Lenard's right, opposite from the rock he rested at.

Marvin turned his gaze toward Lenard. "So…you don't have anything to tell us about that monster."

Lenard matched Marvin's gaze as he furrowed his brow, "What…monster are you talking about?"

Marvin leaned his head back as he copied Lenard's furrowed brow, "The monster using the corpse?"

Lenard's eyes widened, he then quickly changed his gaze. "Oh…yeah, sorry my head is just feeling fuzzy. Something doesn't feel quite right."

Marvin chuckled, "You can say that again. What do you think it was trying to do? Lure us in by making us think it was a person? Why would that?...Well, I guess we almost fell for it. Maybe some people not as clever as us would have."

Lenard nodded as he turned his gaze back to the fire. Marvin did as well. "I wonder if there are any different types of monsters even further out. One could only imagine. Maybe there will be some monsters who look like actual people."

Lenard snickered, "You know…I've heard stories of that before…nursery rhymes I guess."

Marvin smiled as he looked back at Lenard, "Really? From who?"

Lenard raised his arms, "I heard something like that from my mother. I shouldn't talk to strangers because they could be monsters in disguise. It was something she told me just to get me to behave."

Marvin raised an eyebrow, "I thought you were an *Appearer?* How could you know your mother?"

Lenard widened his eyes, "Oh…I uhhh…I remember her from…the other world."

Marvin's mouth gaped, "Really? You had a mother from the other world?! You got to tell me more about that!"

"Sorry, but that's all I really remember," Lenard raised his arms in front of him. Marvin sneered as his eyes leaned to the side and his head tilted.

"Unfortunate…I would have loved to hear more about that," Marvin said.

Lenard laughed, "Maybe I'll remember in the future." He placed his hand on Marvin's back. He took his gaze off of him as he analyzed the camp around him.

Men, women, children, all resided within the camp. Their group was far larger than any Leanrd had seen. He wondered how they managed to keep everything together providing for so many people. Across his view, he saw one man, a man resting at a tree, toward the center bonfire of this camp.

He laid with one leg extended, the other bent and huddled to his chest. His arm wrapped around the bent leg. There was a strange blur that obscured his face. A strange blur because it was entirely blurry, unlike the vague fuzziness he experienced.

He could not distinguish a singular feature residing on his face. Yet, even stranger, was that he still felt the same feeling of familiarity with this man as he did everyone else.

He grew curious of this man, a strange sense of curiosity overpowered him. He kept his gaze fixed on the man as he stood upright..

"Where are you going?" He could hear Marvin asking. He did not answer and approached the blurred man.

As he grew closer, things grew fuzzy and blurry like before. The voices behind him grew muffled. He continued forward. HIs vision grew blurrier, a ringing sound blared his ear drums. He got closer, no farther than two dozen feet away.

The ringing morphed into faint, feminine voices. As his surroundings became blurrier, the man's face did the inverse and became clearer. The feminine voices became audible and screamed 'wake up!' but Lenard continued. He held out his hand, now a few feet away from the man. The face cleared and cleared…and then.

"Wake up!" Two voices shouted at him. He felt his body being shoved around, the blurriness and dizziness he felt from the dream sequence came back in full power, before it faded away.

He jolted upright and glanced around, Jean and Alice surrounded him. Their faces were full of fear and panic and their arms extended onto his body. He raised his hand to his eyes and rubbed eyelids. When he opened his eyes again, everything came into clear view. He noticed tears in Jean and Alice's eyes.

He furrowed his brow, "What the hell is going on?" Alice made a crooked, uneven smile as she lunged herself into Lenard, wrapping her arms around him. Same furrowed expression, Lenard too wrapped his one arm around Alice.

Jean swallowed her tears, "W-we…we saw you collapse…w-we were so scared…we t-thought something happened to you." Lenard's shallow breaths turned deeper.

He groaned, "I'm…fine. I feel okay." Alice released herself from him, crouching back down on her shins. Lenard tucked in his legs and used their voice to stand himself back upright. Jean and Alice stood up with him.

Alice placed her hand on his shoulder, "Are you sure you're okay?" Lenard nodded.

"Give me a play by play of what happened, please," Lenard requested.

Alice pursed her lips, "We were searching for the ground. I heard you place those metal casings into your bag, you stood upright…then just collapsed. We don't know why. You were out for a good ten minutes."

Lenard exhaled as he placed his hand on his heart. "Are you two okay? Nothing happened when I was out, right?"

Alice and Jean glanced at each other. Lenard wrinkled his forehead, "What? What happened?"

"When you went out, and we huddled over you, we saw something…something in the distance. Like a large monster."

"What do you mean, something in the distance? It's pitch-black out there," Lenard raised his forearm, and gestured his hand out to the empty void.

"Whatever it was…it was darker." *The Nothingness.* A chill ran down Lenard's spine. The creature he saw in that first dream sequence? Lenard was unsure what this meant.

"Where did you see it?" He asked.

Alice raised her arm and pointed behind Lenard. "Somewhere over there, it was towering over the trees."

Lenard glanced in the direction she was pointing. Nothing but pitch-black lied in that direction. "Alright, we're getting the hell out of here," Lenard said.

"What about the materials?" Alice asked.

"It doesn't matter, somethings not right here," he said with a sneer on his face. Alice and Jean nodded, he then turned his back to them and retrieved the torch still burrowed into the ground.

He grabbed his bag that laid next to it as well, then wrapped the straps around his shoulders. He walked past Jean and Alice, then waved his hand for them to follow. He heard their footsteps as they began to follow. Before they could leave the district of light from the bonfire, Lenard halted.

The pebble path they had laid, he had thought it seemed different. The pebble path so far was made in a straight line, as per how it usually went. However, he noticed that the pebble path was disarranged. Some pebbles strayed off to dead ends and other pebbles were more than a couple of feet from the point they should have been at. It was almost as if something had tampered with it.

A sickened sense of anxiety struck Lenard. "You two, we need to head back with caution. No talking, understand?" They both nodded their heads. They continued onto the pebble path. Lenard kept a close on the path.

He would on occasion, look back toward Alice and Jean to make sure they were with him. A gasp would leave Alice's mouth each time a loud crackle from the torch would occur. Other than those infrequent noises, a dreadful silence persisted.

As they continued down the path, the more the pebbles returned to normal, his of something being near them grew. He wondered what may have happened if whatever massed with the pebbles attacked the sisters while he was out and he dreaded that possible reality. He quickly re-focused on getting home and realized that now was not the time to be thinking about that.

Alice and Jean's breaths became less shallow. He took that as a sign to relax a little himself, but he wondered though. What was *The Nothingness*? Why did he seem to know about it? Why was he just then placed into another dream sequence? The first time required him to fall asleep, the second he was knocked unconscious.

If it's true that he can enter a dream sequence at any time, then it was not safe for him to be leader. As of right now, he needed to focus on not slipping into that state again until Jean and Alice have been delivered back safe. One question that remained in the back of his head…How did he know *The Nothingness's* name?

Three hours later and the three of them were still traveling across the pebble path. They had grown restless, for one obvious reason, that had not ventured out this far. Lenard did not possess that best sense of time, this he knew. However, there was no possible way they ventured out there in any more time than two hours.

It did not make any damn sense as to why they haven't arrived back to camp yet. Jean and Alice began to shake over an hour ago. A sign of exhaustion as well as terror. He himself began to feel frightened. A result from the combination of strange things that had been happening, as well as the dreadful thought that they might never make it back.

A thought he attempted to keep hidden deep within his mind. If true, they could end up at a long dead end, or follow this path forever.

Just as he was losing hope, far in the distance was a small glimmer of orange light. He gasped when he saw it and altered

Alice and Jean to the orange dot as well. The two of them began to out-pace Lenard and jogged past him.

"Slow down," He demanded. The sisters looked back at him with a pleading look. They nodded and retreated behind him. The small glimmer of light became bigger. The closer they came, the more their sense of safety returned. However, he felt that something still wasn't right.

A slow but creeping emotion wept him. They saw one fire, their camp had three. Maybe the other fires weren't in view yet. That couldn't be it, he was able to see the three fires for quite a distance before they vanished.

Was this another camp? That couldn't be, the trail they made should lead them back to theirs. They hadn't come across any other camps during that time.

While he could hear Alice and Jean growing excited from noises they made, his stomach began to sink. "Guys…be careful, I don't think that's our camp."

The sister's noises ceased. "What do you mean? What other camp could it be?" Alice asked.

"I'm not sure, just keep your head up," Lenard said. The fire came closer, tents became visible, voices became audible. There were people there. As they grew closer, tents came into view. Few people there, as none were in view themselves. They were no more than a dozen feet away when Lenard heard a clicking sound.

"Stop There!" A strangely familiar voice called out. The three of them stopped in their tracks, not daring to move a muscle. "Who are you?" The voice asked.

"We're venturers, we think we may have gotten lost," Lenard said.

"Lost? What do you mean lost? You with another group?" The man asked.

"Yes. We laid a pebble path on our venture. However, it seems we may have stumbled on a different path. We mean no harm, it's only us three here!" Lenard claimed.

"How do I know I can trust you?" The voice asked.

Lenard snickered, "We're all friends in *The Forest*, aren't we?"

The voice laughed, "I thought that once…I was mistaken."

Lenard sneered, "Look…we aren't here to do anything, why don't you come out so we can talk face to face…we'll both get a better idea of who we're talking to."

The voice scoffed, "So I can get ambushed. Is that your plan?"

"God dammit man, we just need help!" Lenard shouted.

"I don't give a damn what you need." Lenard knew this kind of distrust very well. Back when he was on his own, when he was with Hamon. He heard the voice sigh, "...Do you have any weapons on you?"

"I have a crowbar. The girl to my left has a dagger," he gestured toward Alice.

"Lay them both on the ground, a couple feet in front of you." Lenard nodded as he laid down his backpack. He unzipped it, metal casings clashed against each other. He stuck his hand in and grasped it on the crowbar then pulled it out and threw it away from him, toward the direction of the voice.

He turned his hip to Alice and held out his hand. Alice gave him a worried look. Lenard stared at her for a couple of seconds. She reached toward her belt and sheathed the dagger.

She placed it in Lenard's hand, who turned back and threw it with the crowbar.

"See…no more weapons. Now can we talk…" A rustling noise came from the bushes, then footsteps traveled near them.

A wooden rod first entered into the light circling them. Down the wooden rod, outlined with metal, came an iron sight similar to the pistol.

It was the musket…he had no doubt about it, but there was something else that rocked his senses even more. The man's face came into view.

Lenard froze in place…thousands of different thoughts traversed his mind. He knew this face, he's seen it before.

He gulped, "Wha…My name's Lenard…what's yours?" He shivered, afraid of the answer he knew would come.

"It's Marvin," The voice answered.

Chapter 12

No Time To Spare

Hamon gazed upward upon a tower of stone bricks that he had laid. A circular tower that surrounded a new firepit in a wall of stone. He felt proud of his handiwork and glanced back at Klyde with a smile, who shared that smile with him. Picc stood behind him, he kept his gaze focused on the piece of paper.

"This is well made. It honestly turned out better than I could have hoped. Well done, Hamon," Picc said.

"No problem," Hamon placed his hand on the back of his head. He glanced upward as he scanned the camp. "Why isn't Lenard back yet? He should be back by now. It's making me worried."

"Lenard might just be taking his time. He's not the type to rush through things," Klyde said.

"Yeah…but he's not the type that likes to make other people worry either. Especially when he has the sisters with him."

"I'm sure they'll be back soon. We shouldn't worry ourselves too much. Like you said, Lenard probably wouldn't like that."

Hamon gave a nod but couldn't help but feel worried. A small sign of regret plagued him. Maybe he had rushed Lenard too quickly into being an expedition leader.

Picc stepped forward and passed Hamon, then halted right at the wall of stone. He took out a lighter from his left pocket and stuck his hand in the small rectangular opening a couple feet from the bottom.

"It's time we get this thing started," He activated the lighter and left his hand sitting there for a few seconds, then the wood within ignited. Picc pulled out his hand and took a few steps back and ended up next to Hamon.

He turned his gaze to him, "So…this thing will help to make the flashlight?"

Picc smiled, "Correct. Although we'll probably have to make some bellows in order to make it hot enough to melt iron."

"Sounds like a lot more work," Hamon sighed.

"That's what you have to do when making something that doesn't exist in this world," Picc smirked.

Hamon heard a group of footsteps coming from behind him. He turned to see Quinton, Mark and Jarold enter back into the camp. They were sent on an expedition not too long ago for material collection.

Hamon sneered as Quinton approached. "What's with the face? You aren't happy to see me?" Quinton asked.

"No…I was just expecting Lenard. He left before you guys did, and he's still not back." Quinton nodded. "You…didn't happen to see him out there, did you?" Hamon asked.

"No, I thought he might have been back already," Quinton said.

Hamon shook his head, "Anyway, how did it go? You didn't have any trouble taking the leadership role, did you?"

"I was a little worried, but we ended up fine. I'm sure Lenard is too, only time could tell," Quinton said with a nervous smile. "In good news, I've got a rare find that could prove to be very useful."

"What is it?" Quinton slid down the straps of his bag and placed it onto the ground. He opened the zipper and pulled out a large spool of rope.

"Thirty-five feet of rope. One of the largest finds I think we've ever made for length of rope." Picc walked past Hamon with a smile on his face, then took the spool of rope out of Quinton's hands.

"This is perfect, how much rope does that make in total?" He asked.

"We should have somewhere around seventy-five feet of rope," Hamon replied.

Picc's smile widened, "That's perfect, we have all the rope we need. What else do you have?"

Quinton grabbed his bag from the straps and turned it upside down, laying out all of its contents on the ground. "Just about everything else you asked for. That should be everything we need."

Picc shook Quinton's hand, "Great job!" He was too elated to see it, but Hamon thought it mighty convenient that Quinton was able to find all of those materials in one search. Especially the length of rope.

Years Hamon has been going on expeditions. He's pillaged countless camps. The amount of times he has found a length of rope above thirty feet could be counted on his fingers. The odds had to be at least a one in a thousand. It was all just too convenient.

"I'm going to go eat. I don't think I've had anything in the past twenty hours," Hamon sighed as he turned his sight to Klyde.

Klyde nodded, "I'll keep watch over here then." Hamon waved to him as he walked away and headed toward the unoccupied edge campfire. As he did, he stopped by a tent that was along the way. He crouched toward the oak chest that rested next to it.

He opened, inside rested MREs stacked on top of each other. Littered over them were utensils like spoons. Hamon grabbed one of the packs resting on the top as well as a spoon. He shut the chest. A loud slam echoed through the camp.

He took the MRE to the edge campfire. Once at the fire, he picked up the metal fire poker, and stuck it through the slit hole at the top of the pack, then positioned it over the fire and let it rest there.

The zipper of a tent a dozen feet away from him opened. Out of it Amber crawled. She glanced around and her eyes met Hamon, then approached him. Her body came into the light of the bonfire. Her eyes were tired, hair disheveled and her clothes wrinkled.

Hamon gave her a wide smile, "You've been getting rest?"
"No," She answered, then she sat herself down next to Hamon, staying awkwardly quiet.

Hamon scoffed, "Well, you hungry? I wouldn't mind sharing this MRE with you." She shook her head. He pulled the MRE out of the fire and grabbed onto the bottom carefully so as to not burn his hand, then ripped open the top that created a slit.

The delicious smell of smoke poured out of it. He took a deep whiff of it as he too sat down and stuck the spoon through the slit and scooped out a portion of broth.

"I thought you were on my side," Amber spoke softly. Hamon glanced toward her as he raised his eyebrow. "What do you mean?"

Amber scoffed, "I see you out there, helping them put together whatever the hell that ugly tower is. I thought you were on my side…the rational side. The side that actually wants to take the time to process Kaylee's death."

Hamon sighed as he leaned his head back, "I'm not on their side. I'm still on yours. But we both agree that Picc is an enemy. Other members of the camp don't see it that way. My best bet is to at least know what he is up to."

Amber glared at him, "And do you? Has all the information you've gathered made all of the contributions you've done for them been worth it." He clenched his fist because was still unsure as to what Picc was planning.

He knew this stuff was going toward making a flashlight, but he still did not know how it will be done. "Hey…I remember it was you who told me the saying, keep your friends close and your enemies closer."

Amber snickered, "To me, it sounds more like, if you can't beat them, join them."

"Whatever damn saying you want. It doesn't matter, what I am trying to do stays the same," Hamon waved his hand.

"And what is that exactly?" She questioned.

"I just told you. I'm trying to see what he's up to," Hamon gestured his arms out wide.

"And why are you trying to do that?"

"What?...uh…because I want to keep this group safe. That's why," Hamon said.

Amber smirked, "Is that what you think you're doing? Keeping us safe?"

Hamon sneered, "Yes, that's exactly what I am doing."

Amber quivered, "Kaylee is dead…I haven't had a single thought that wasn't suicidal since then. Lenard and the sisters have been gone for hours. And you are playing spy with the person who started all of this. You call *that*…keeping us safe."

Hamon threw his hands in the air, "I call it trying the best I fucking can! I don't like this any more than you do. But what choice do we have?!"

"I don't know…just…do something," She pleaded.

His gaze softened as his sight fell, "I know…and I'm trying. But you need to give me some time."

Amber nodded. She held her head down as she sniffled. He bit his lip and re-clenched his fist, "I'm sorry for yelling. I just…I'm just trying to figure out what the hell is going on right now. Once Lenard comes back…we'll…do something for Kaylee. We'll take a break from making this damn flashlight. What are those things called?...those…things you do to mourn someone's death, in the other world."

"Funerals…" She said softly.

Hamon nodded, "Right…we'll have one of those for her…when Lenard gets back." Hamon dug his spoon back into the broth and filled his mouth with the broth again. Not another word was spoken.

Lenard stood and faced a person he thought could not exist until now. A man that shouldn't exist. The blonde hair, the blue eyes and the muscular build…he could tell exactly who it was. *Marvin*. But how? How is this possible? he wondered.

Marvin kept his gun pointed at Lenard, who made no action as to not set him off. This was Marvin, but he was different. His eyes were colder, his expression more blank.

He also now possessed a beard, something he did not have in Lenard's dream sequence. His body was stiff. Lenard thought to call him out by name. However, it seems Marvin does not recognize Lenard, as he should and if he called him by name, he might panic.

"Please sir, we just need help," Alice begged. Lenard reached his arm and laid his hand flat in front of her.

"Calm down, I can handle this," he said. Marvin lowered his gun, then inspected them one last time to confirm they were indeed not with anyone or had any weapons on them.

He glanced up at Lenard, "Follow me." He turned his back to them and walked toward the bonfire in the distance. Lenard turned his hip toward the sisters. Their expressions seemed uncertain.

"Come on," Lenard waved his hand as he began to follow the man. The sisters tagged along not much later. The campsite was feeble compared to the camp Lenard saw in his dream. There was only one tent, a singular oak chest beside it. The fire itself was small. The flames burned low and the wood was mostly ash at this point.

A fire that would not last much longer without kindling, Lenard thought. A horizontal log rested on the opposite side of the tent from the fire. The oak wood was rotted and had a large gash on the edge.

Marvin pointed toward the log, “You three go ahead and have a seat…I’ll prepare some food.” Lenard nodded as he led the sisters to the log with him. The three of them sat, Lenard in the middle, Alice to his right and Jean to his left.

Across from them was Marvin, who was digging through the now open chest next to the tent. A realization had just hit Lenard as he did so. Marvin…the one at this camp is him. There were no signs of anyone else living here. He was on his own. Lenard thought no one could survive on their own other than him.

Jean turned her head toward him, “What the hell is going on? Why did our pebble path lead us here?”

Lenard sighed, “I have no idea. Let’s just work with this guy until we can find our way back.”

Alice placed her hands on his shoulder, “How are we going to do that? The pebble path doesn’t lead us back home.”

“We’ll find a way. We probably just got our paths mixed up. We’ll backtrack and try to find the correct path,” Lenard said as he grasped her hands and took them off of him.

“What’s that weapon that he has? It looks like the pistol,” Jean noted.

“I think it's the musket,” Lenard said.

The sisters both gasped, “You think that’s it? Really!?” Alice whispered loudly.

“Keep your voice down,” Lenard scolded.

Alice raised her forearms, “Okay…but if that’s the musket…then that’s huge for us. We finally found it.” A smile on the sister’s faces widened.

Lenard scoffed, "And how do you suppose we do that? The musket he has belongs to him. We're not going to steal it."

Jean shrugged, "Maybe…we could talk him into joining our group. You did notice that he's out here on his own, didn't you. I'm sure he's dying to have a group to be with."

Leanrd bit his lip. If only she knew how wrong she was, he thought. It took Hamon months to bond with him back when his old group first discovered him. Marvin doesn't look any better himself…but maybe he could do it.

Afterall, he did have some amount of knowledge on Marvin. Maybe he could use his past to convince him. Marvin stood up from the chest with a couple packs of MREs and spoons.

"Sorry that took me a while…I don't have an organized chest system," Marvin said.

Lenard raised his palms, "Don't worry about it…and you don't have to feed us, we have our own packs of MREs."

Marvin chuckled, "These aren't for you."

Lenard responded with a sneer. Marvin crouched down on the opposite side of the fire and grabbed the fire poker that laid next to him. He inserted the poker through the slit of the pack and stuck it above the fire.

"So…would you be able to help us find our way back? To our campsite?" Lenard asked.

Marvin raised an eyebrow, "Why can't you find it yourself? Don't you have it mapped?" Lenard furrowed his brow.

Marvin did mention something about mapping in his dream sequence. He never got any of the details of that, however. “Uhh…I don’t quite know what that is.”

“I should have figured,” Marvin scoffed. He turned his hip toward the tent and reached for a bag that laid at the entrance of it, then grabbed it by its straps and dragged it next to him.

He opened the zipper. A piece of paper was pulled out. Marvin unfolded the paper. The size was somewhere around thirty-six inch by thirty-six inch. The largest piece of paper Lenard had ever seen.

Marvin angled the fire poker into the ground so the MRE would still be above the flames. He stood up with the paper in hand and approached the three of them. Once next to them, he faced away with a drawing on the graph now displayed to them. It was an outline of the forest. Along with various dotted lines and X’s.

“This is a map…those lines and X’s are paths I traveled and campsites I’ve come across,” He pointed toward a circle that was dotted two-thirds down the map. “That’s where we are,” He slid his finger downward. “That’s where you were…maybe even a bit further. The range outside this map is what we like to call…the outer woods.”

Lenard raised his eyebrow, “And what the hell is the outer woods?”

A confident, near arrogant smile formed on Marvin’s face, “A place of pure hell. Monster’s like you’ve never seen before. Creatures of your worst nightmares. For some reason they don’t come into, what we call, the inhabited woods. We theorized the reason why they didn’t was because of the mass population within the inhabited woods.

The mass amounts of fires probably keep them away. This map marks an area of around five hundred by five-hundred miles. A twenty-five hundred mile area."

"Five hundred miles…that doesn't seem right. We we're attempting to head back to our camp…we only journeyed for an hour or two. We shouldn't have made it any more than a couple of miles," Lenard explained.

"Hmph…perhaps you may have been teleported," Marvin proposed. Lenard snickered. Marvin glared at him, "I'm being serious here. There have been rumors about a monster capable of teleporting people in the outer woods."

Jean quickly raised her hand to get Marvin's attention. Both him and Lenard turned their gaze to her. "Do you know anything about a very large monster…one that's darker than pitch black." Lenard turned his head back to find Marvin nodding.

"*The Nothingness*…that's what we called it. It's what wiped out my previous group. It lurks on the edge of the outer woods," he explained.

Lenard furrowed his brow, "W-wait…you've come across it?" Marvin bobbed his head up and down. "How did you survive?"

He lifted his index finger, "It has one weakness, *fire*. When it attacked, I managed to burn one of its legs. Some of our group was able to escape…others were not so lucky. I'm not completely sure who managed to survive. But most likely not many."

Picc…Lenard wondered if he was one of the venturers of that attack. He must have been. Lenard thought there must be a way to get more answers without attracting suspicion.

"So…this…*Nothingness*. If it attacked your campsite, does that mean your campsite was in the outer woods?"

Marvin shook his head, "No…we were close, but we were still in the inhabited woods."

"But I thought you said monsters like those don't come into the inhabited woods?" Lenard asked.

"Yes…I don't know why it did. It could be that we were close enough to the edge for the monster to attack us anyway. I…I think it was lured. I don't have any proof of this…only that we began to spot it getting closer and closer to us. On occasions," Marvin said.

"Wait…in the outer woods…are there monsters that use bodies as decoys?" Lenard questioned.

"Ahh…so you have been to the outer woods before. Back when our group was in our prime, we would stumble across those monsters from time to time," Marvin said.

"Sounds like your old group was quite accomplished," Alice said.

Mavin smirked, "It was a utopia. A group of twenty-six people. We had gadgets and tools no other group had. We were a monopoly. Even…a utopia like that could be crushed in a single night by what lies out there."

"Hold on, before we switch the subject…how did you spot the monsters who used bodies as decoys?" Lenard asked.

"Hmm," Marvin whispered as he turned his hip back to his bag. Out from it he grabbed a cylinder shaped object made of metal. At the end of a clear object, embedded within it. Marvin pointed the object to his side and pressed a button that rested on it. Out from the clear part shot a beam light.

Lenard realized, "Hey…that's a flashlight, right?"

Marvin nodded, “I’m surprised you know about it? Where did you find it?”

“We’re building one…Picc told us that the flashlight didn’t exist within *the forest*…so how do you have one?” Alice asked.

Marvin’s eyes widened and his mouth gaped. A spike of panic struck Lenard. Marvin stood up from where he stood. “Girl…tell me how it is you know that man. Now.”

Chapter 13

Sneaking Suspicion

Hamon watched as Picc used the fire poker in order to insert a bunch of metal casings into the fire. He had grown restless for almost a full day and Lenard and the sisters had still not returned. He stood with his arms crossed, the tip of his foot taping the ground. He glared at Picc, who paid no mind to him. Klyde stood next to him, although he stood much more still.

Once the metal casings were inserted, Picc stepped away from the furnace. He gazed at his handiwork as the metal within began to heat. "Give it a couple of hours in there…and it will be soft enough to make something out of it."

"I think you're forgetting something," Hamon said. Picc glanced back at him with an irritated expression.

"I'm aware that Lenard still has not returned. Once the flashlight has been made, we'll go look after him," Picc said. His lack of worry had started to piss him off.

Hamon sneered, "We should be looking for him now. Who the hell knows what could be happening to him."

Klyde placed his hand on Hamon's shoulder, "Weren't you the one who said Lenard could handle himself as a leader?"

"And I stand by that, but that doesn't mean he isn't in any danger. You of all people should know that Klyde," Hamon scoffed.

Klyde glared at him, "You don't think I have concern over my own group member. I know Lenard could be in danger. Rushing out there isn't going to do any good for us." Hamon turned his head away with that same sneer plastering his face.

He had thought of going after Lenard himself, maybe with Mark or Quinton. However, Quinton seemed a bit suspicious to him and Mark was busy putting together the artificial river with Jarold. There was only one person who could help him…Amber.

He walked away from Picc and Klyde and approached Amber's tent on the edge of camp. Once outside it he loudly whispered; "Amber!"

"....What?" She answered.

"Could you come out here for a second? I have something I want to ask you," Hamon said.

He could hear Amber scoff as shuffling could be heard. The zipper to the tent opened and laid.

on her knees was Amber. Her hair was even more disheveled and her expression even more tired.

"Sorry to wake you…I just…I need to talk with you." Amber stared at him for a brief moment, then she sighed and exited her tent. She walked past him and sat herself down by the fire.

Hamon approached and sat next to her. "So…Lenard and the sisters are still missing." Amber nodded. "I…want to go look for them. I tried talking about it with Klyde and Picc, but neither of them would listen. Everyone else is either too busy or too inexperienced to venture with me. I…was wondering if you would come to help me look for them."

"So now you want to be on my side," she placed her hand on her chest in a manner that suggested sarcasm.

"I've always been on your side. Look…I'm sorry for those things I said to you earlier. You're going through a hard time and you don't deserve to be treated like that. But this is serious…I need your help. For all we know Lenard and the sisters could be dying. Us going out there and finding them could be their only hope," Hamon said.

"Hmm…and what if they are already dead? Is it…really worth it?" Amber questioned. A fair presumption. However, something in Hamon's chest told him that this was not the truth.

"Lenard managed to survive on his own in *the forest* for years. I'm sure he's still alive. And I'm sure he's kept the sisters alive as well," Hamon claimed.

Amber sighed, "Fine…I'll come. But I'm not doing it for your sake. I'm doing it for Lenard and the sisters."

"That's exactly what I wanted to hear. Now, I don't think Klyde is going to just let us leave. We'll need a way to distract him and prepare without him noticing."

"You can leave that to me. You retrieve supplies from the other edge of the camp," she said as she placed her hand on her chest. He nodded again. The two of them stood on their feet, then he walked straight for the other edge, with Amber following next to him.

He passed Klyde and Picc. Amber halted when she stood close to Klyde. She fell out of Hamon's sight. On the other side of the camp was Jarold and Mark. They had been putting together a wooden structure.

It was a sort of slide. A wooden plank laid flat, angled slightly into the air on one side. Wooden walls around a foot high surrounded the flat wood.

The walls of the lowest portion stood three feet tall. A rubber hose was connected to one end of the structure and looped to the other. Mark was on the lowest end, where he tinkered with the rubber hose. Jarold was on the other end and made sure that the wood pillars angling the plank weren't prone to snapping.

The structure itself rested three dozen feet away from the edge campfire. In a new flat area created due to the removal of trees. The structure itself was quite large, being about fifteen feet long and three feet wide. Jarold and Mark's focus on the structure made it easy to walk past them without them having noticed.

He approached a chest that lied two feet away from the edge campfire and opened it. The hinges creaked as he did.

Within it were packets of MREs stacked on top of each other. It was their secondary food chest. He grabbed three MREs in each hand, then turned his hip and set them on the ground next to him.

He turned back to the chest and carefully closed it. A quiet thump was made when the flat lid smacked close. Not too far away were a couple of bags that lied organized next to a tent.

He stood up and grabbed two of the bags and opened their zippers. The MREs were placed within. He re-zipped the bag. Now all he needed were some tools and water flasks.

The problem was that the only chest where water flasks were stored was the two of the four chests in the center. Where Hamon saw Klyde and Amber were still discussing with each other. There was one chest where its view was now obscured due to the pillar of stone.

However, even if Hamon managed to reach that chest without being seen, his hatchet was in the tent closest to Klyde. There was no possible way for him to retrieve it without Klyde having noticed him. He could provide a simple excuse as to why he needed it, but he knew that would not be enough to convince Klyde.

He kept himself focused on one task at a time. First, he needed to find a way to that water flask chest. Before he could even formulate a plan, the clunky noise of the metal lid being taken off of a flask could be heard.

He turned his gaze in that direction. Next to Jarold, on the side of the structure facing Hamon, laid over twenty flasks of water. Almost half of their entire supply. It must have been for the artificial river. The flasks were organized in a neat pattern of four rows of five. Jarold stood next to them as he held two in his hand, then poured the contents of the flask into the structure.

Hamon approached him, “Hey.”

Jarold turned around to see him. “Oh, Hamon. Uhh…whatcha talkin 'to me for?” The flasks were emptied and Jarold pulled them away and set them next to him on the opposite side of the full flasks.

Hamon halted a couple feet away from him, “Picc miscounted the amount of materials we’re going to need. He wants me to go on another expedition for materials. We're going to need some water for that."

Jarold raised his eyebrow, "Why don't you just get it from the chest?"

He placed his hand on the back of his head. "I figured since I was here already I might as well take some flasks off your hand," he said.

"We might need all of these flasks. This river is going to need a lot of water," Jarold scoffed.

"Quit being such an ass about it and just hand me some damn flasks," Hamon said.

"How many do you need?" Jarold rolled his eyes. Even in times like this he still had to be a pain in the ass, Hamon thought to himself.

"Six," Hamon answered. Jarold sighed as he scooped three flasks in each hand. He lifted his arms toward Hamon who grasped onto the flasks. Hamon reached toward his back, opened the zipper with his free fingers and slipped the flasks within.

Jarold furrowed his brow, "Who are you going with?"

Hamon slid his eyes to the side, "Amber and I."

"Amber's going venturing again? Is she okay? I mean…the last time she went venturing was over five years ago," Jarold said.

Hamon smiled, "She's doing okay for herself. I'm sure she'll be okay. I think she wants to do this to get all this off her mind." Jarold nodded. He truly did believe Amber was looking for something to keep her mind occupied, as mad as she is with Klyde for doing the same thing.

"Now get the hell out of here so we can work," Jarold waved him away.

Hamon snickered. "Try not to work yourself to death," he said as he walked past them and back toward the center fire. Now the only thing he needed was his hatchet. Thoughts of how to get his hatchet circulated through Hamon's mind.

He could tell Klyde that he only wants to clean it, but then the two bags on his back would look suspicious. Perhaps telling him that he was off to get more wood.

Picc was next to him however, he would tell them they didn't need any more. Maybe Amber could simply keep him distracted enough for him to sneak behind him. No…not even she was that good at keeping him distracted. He could always use a different tool. His hatchet was what he was best trained with, however there were a plethora of other tools that littered the camp.

The dagger…it was the closest thing to his hatchet that he could get without having attracted.

Klyde's suspicion. It rested in the tent next to the one Amber had laid in, on the other edge of camp.

All Hamon had to do was traverse to the other side traveling along the edge of the camp on the side Klyde was facing away from. When he made it to the other side he opened that tent, retrieved the dagger, and placed it on his belt.

He gazed over to Amber who was still talking with Klyde. She glanced over to him once she noticed him. He dipped his head and gave her the signal that they were good to go.

He could see Amber point her fingers to her side as she began to walk away from Klyde. She made her way to Hamon.

“Got everything?” She asked. Hamon nodded. “How long are we going to be searching for them?”

“I got us three MREs and water flasks each. That should last us a day and a half.”

Amber shook her head, “We’ll make it last three days.”

“Uhh…are you sure about that, we’ll be starving,” Hamon said.

“They probably are too,” she said. She was right. They had no right to be concerned over their own hunger when Lenard or the sisters could be on the verge of death.

“Right…three days then. We’ll follow along the pebble path that they made.” Amber nodded. He turned toward the abyss. The two of them walked past the fire out to the edge of the camp. Right at the edge was a path of gray pebbles leading out into the darkness. Amber lifted her arm toward Hamon, as he turned his hip to face her. She grasped a lantern between her fingers.

He took the lantern from her hands. He took one last look back toward the camp as they both began walking.

Lenard sat with his hands rested on his thighs. An awkward silence persisted. Across from them, Marvin sat with his hands interlocked and covering his mouth. Finally, he sighed.

“So…how long has Picc been with your group now?” Lenard, Alice and Jean looked amongst themselves. Lenard turned his gaze back to Marvin.

“I would say around two months now,” Lenard said. It was a general estimate. There was no way to measure how long it had been since they had gotten lost. For all he could know it could have been much longer.

Marvin chuckled, "That bastard, he must have been with other groups as well during that time, huh? I can't believe it, he really had me going thinking he was dead. I suppose he probably thinks the same fate of me. I shouldn't be surprised with that ability of his and all."

"Uhh…are you talking about how he could see the other world?" Jean asked. Marvin nodded.

"We were pretty far ahead of the survival game than most people. We had good tools and equipment, lots of people, lots of land. Even so, when Picc first came into our camp, we discovered so much more. I'm not surprised you folks want him for yourselves," he laughed.

"So…were you good friends with Picc? Back when he was with your group." Marvin nodded as a smile rested on his face.

"He would tell me tales of the other world. I was a lot younger back then, I won't lie. Those stories got me excited. It was like…for the first time, there was something in the forest that was fun," Marvin claimed.

Lenard felt a strange sense of confusion. Picc really had not lied about who he was. He is someone who could see the other world. That meant all of that doubt Lenard placed on him was wrong.

He sighed. Marvin noticed the displeasure over his face, "S'wrong, good friend? Down in the dumps about something?"

Lenard shook his head. "Don't worry about me…it's nothing." Marvin lifted his head. He turned his gaze toward his bag, reaching into it once more. Out of it he pulled a small hand sized, rectangular container.

The top part opened up. Marvin pulled out little sticks of white paper with orange at one end. He placed the orange end in his mouth, then reached to his side where a lighter was placed.

He lifted the lighter toward his mouth and lit the other end of the paper stick. An orange hue illuminated the end. Marvin inhaled, then removed the paper stick from his mouth and blew out smoke.

Lenard furrowed his brow. Marvin glanced up at him, "What? Never had a cig before?" Lenard shook his head. Marvin reached back down for the small box and pulled out another. He lifted it with his two fingers in Lenard's direction.

"Why don't you try it out." Lenard stood still for a moment, considering if he should take one or not, then he kneeled toward Marvin and took the cig from his hand. He placed the orange end in his mouth same as Marvin, who passed the lighter to his hand. He raised it toward the cig in his mouth and ignited the end. He inhaled the smoke.

A bitter taste entered his mouth, a metallic feeling littered his tongue. He pulled the cig from his mouth, placed his hand on his chest and began to cough.

"That's how my first experience was." Marvin laughed.

Lenard whipped a tear from his eye, "What the hell is this thing?" The taste was never like anything he had tasted before. He struggled to describe it in his own head. The closest thing he could compare it to was that time he had eaten ash as a dare.

Marvin removed his cig, "It's a cigarette. You'll find quite a few packs when you enter into the outer woods. The farther you travel out there, the more other world items you'll find. I made a habit out of smoking these things during my many expeditions to the outer woods."

Lenard placed the cig back in his mouth. He inhaled once more. The same bitter taste plagued his mouth, only this time being met with a strange sensation. A sort of pull that made him want to smoke it even more. "So, you've traveled out to the outer woods on multiple occasions. Why? I thought you said the risk was greater out there," he asked.

"But so are the rewards. It's like an addiction. You can't get yourself to stop going after you do it once. The amount of goods that littered those lands are almost enough to completely trump the horrors of what lies out there."

Lenard blew out a stream of smoke as he inhaled again. "What kind of goods are out there?"

"Well, for one, the musket is one thing you can find right at the border of the outer woods. I found it after our group was slaughtered. I'm sure Picc has told you this, but he claims that whatever exists in the other world doesn't exist in the forest, correct?" Marvin asked.

Jean shot up from her seat, "How did you know?"

"What he says is technically true, but it's not the full truth. Whatever exists in the other world you can't find in the inhabitable woods…but you can in the outer woods."

Jean gasped as Alice and Lenard's eyes widened. "Things like high caliber guns, machines, vehicles, all could be found in the outer woods. The farther you get out, the more other world items you come across. I've never come across any of those things myself, but I've heard tales."

"From who?" Lenard asked.

Marvin raised his hand in the air, "A fella named Jacob. He had a photographic memory. His group accidentally ventured far out into the outer woods when he was a boy. He could vividly describe everything he came across. Even with the horrifying monsters of the outer woods. With the materials they stumbled upon they survived for a good while."

"Hold on…if Picc knows about the outer woods then why hasn't he told us anything about it," Alice stated.

Marvin shrugged, "To keep you safe. Any good man would. When I say the outer woods are an addiction, I mean that as literally as I can. Even if *The Nothingness* gets you, something will, maybe even something far more terrifying."

That would not make sense. If there really were items from the other world in the outer woods, Picc would have done anything to get there. It's not like he was the type of person who'd wince at sacrificing a member.

"Hold on," Jean said. "If goods from the other world appear more frequently the farther out you go in the outer woods. Does that mean the other world could potentially reside beyond those woods?"

Marvin flicked his now finished cig into the fire. "That's a possibility. But you'd have to travel thousands of miles to find out. That kind of journey on foot could take years."

"But do you think it's impossible?" She asked while she clenched her fists. Marvin closed his eyes and raised his face upwards.

"One in a million," He dipped his head and faced her. "I would wager you would have to be one in a million to make it out that far. That's even if the other world really does reside out there."

Jean grunted. Marvin smirked, "That's the true misfortune of life. The best things it has to offer are the things it offers the least." Alice stood up and sat next to her sister. She wrapped her arm around her and pushed her to lean on her shoulder.

"I don't say that to put you down kid. Back when I was your age I thought about the same thing. But hey…at least there's something to live for," Marvin said. Lenard glanced back at the sister's. Jean was whipping a small tear from her eye.

"Maybe we should all get some sleep before we attempt to find our way home. You two are probably all tuckered out from today's expedition anyway," Lenard said. Alice glanced at Lenard and nodded her head.

"Well, shit…I don't have any extra tents," Marvin said.

Lenard waved his hand, "Don't worry about that. We'll sleep out here. We'll be out of your hair in a couple of hours."

"I wish you folks a safe journey home. I'll even lend you my map if you'd like," he gestured his hand toward the large paper.

Lenard shook his head, "Thanks, but we'll manage." Marvin lifted his hand and stood up. He turned toward the tent and leaned over to unzip it, then entered and re-zipped it from the inside.

Lenard and the sisters stood up. He went over to the left to a tree a couple feet away from the fire. The sisters laid themselves down on a stone on the opposite side. Even across the fire Lenard was able to keep a close eye on them. Nothing like that massive camp he saw in those dream sequences. This camp was claustrophobic. There was a weird sense of sorrow to it.

Chapter 14

What Awaits

A bonfire rested in the center of Hamon's view. He sat there and gazed into it. His knees bent toward his chest, his arms wrapped around them. In his peripheral vision was a tent. Amber was currently resting within.

They had endlessly walked across the pebble path, for hours and hours, and still no sign of Lenard or the sisters. Why had Lenard continued forth so far? He knew he should have been out there for only a couple of hours. Had it…happened again, Hamon thought. An old behavior back in the old days when Lenard first came into Hamon's old group. Due to the side effects of isolation within the forest for so long, Lenard developed…some issues.

After a year with Hamon's old group, Lenard had kicked the habit. But he himself was fearful that it could come back at any time. Hamon always doubted that. However, this situation wouldn't make any sense unless he did.

He placed his hand on the back of his head and rubbed it as he sighed. If Lenard is out there, he'll find him. Then the sound of shuffling came from inside the tent. The zipper opened as Amber crawled out. Her eye bags weren't as deep, she might have gotten some proper sleep. She stood up and approached him, then sat down next to him. She extended her legs and crossed them over each other.

Hamon turned his gaze to her, "You could have gotten more sleep, you know. We aren't heading out for another hour."

"I got more than enough rest. We should be out there looking for them. Not resting and taking our time. They could be dying," She groaned.

He placed his hand on her shoulder, "And if we don't get proper rest we're going to end up dying."

She brought in her legs as she hunched over them. "I hate this…I wish everything could just go back to the way it was. Back before…Picc showed up."

Hamon snickered, "Even if some won't say it, I think we all wish for that. But this is just how it all played out. The best thing we could do is at least make sure we don't go wishing things were like how they are right now."

Amber nodded. He turned his sight back to the fire. The hypnotizing gaze of the flames made it easy to enter deep into thought.

"Hey," Amber interrupted.

Hamon side eyed her, "What is it?"

"Where do you think we go when we die?" She asked.

Hamon furrowed his brow, "What's this about?"

"I don't know…I just want to talk about it. Where do you think we go when we die?" Amber shrugged.

Hamon placed his hand on his chin. "I always thought it was eternal rest. An unending moment passing in an instant."

"Hmm…I always liked to believe we crossed into the other world when we die. Maybe that's how *Appearers* came about. Maybe they were people in the other world who died and came here," Amer said.

"You think this is hell?" Hamon smirked.

"What else could it be? But…if there's a hell, maybe there's a god too," she gestured toward the sky.

Hamon's smirk turned into a smile, "A god, huh?"

Amber smiled as she wrapped her forearm on the back of her neck, "Yeah…and maybe when Kaylee died…he saw how much she loved the other world, so he sent her there. I remember slight glimpses of faith in god from the other world.

I never put too much stock in it…I mean, what kind of god puts his people in a hell like this. But I won't lie…I…I couldn't help but pray these past couple days. That…maybe Kaylee at least made it out of here."

"Then…would you mind if I pray with you. Two messages are bound to make her chances better than one," Hamon offered.

Amber looked at him with a deep smile. She turned her gaze to the fire as she closed her eyes and placed the palm of her hands together. Hamon watched and followed her movement.

"Oh lord…please…let Kaylee make it to the other world."

A long treacherous path laid ahead of Lenard. If it's true that he and the sisters were teleported, that means he could be as far away as five hundred miles away from home. That could take several weeks to travel. Not even the grand expedition was that long.

Beside him were the sisters. They were filling their bags with supplies that Marvin welcomed them to take. MREs, water flasks and a new torch. Lenard held it in his right hand, his other placed on the strap of his bag. Marvin sat by the fire and watched them prepare to venture back out. He and Lenard had some discussion on where his camp might be.

They both came to the conclusion that his campsite was somewhere around the top right corner of the map. Marvin's campsite was at the bottom center. It was not a precise measure, but it was all they had to go off of.

Lenard glanced at Marvin, he was grasping onto a glass bottle with his right hand. Lenard approached him as he burrowed the torch in the ground. He stopped a couple feet away from him.

"Hey, thank you for helping us out, we appreciate it," he said.

Marvin smirked, "It's no issue, when you're on your own you really don't need that much food and water."

Lenard laughed, "Yeah, I get what you mean by that. I was on my own for a long time as well."

"You were?" Marvin asked while he raised an eyebrow.

Lenard nodded, "From the time I was a toddler to my teens, I spent all those years surviving on my own."

Marvin placed his hand on the back of his head. "Damn, sorry to hear about that." He took another sip from the bottle.

"Yeah…but eventually, I found people. Mainly my friend, Hamon. When our old group first found me, I didn't play too nice with them. Only he argued to keep me around," he said.

"Sounds like a good man," Marvin smiled.

Lenard smiled too as he took his seat with him. "He sure is. You'd like our current group, they're nice people. We don't always see eye to eye, but we always have each other's backs."

Marvin dipped his head, "I know what you're trying to do."

"Then why don't you?" Lenard questioned.

"I lost one group already…the strongest group. What's the point of going to some other…weaker group, and have the same thing happen all over again," Marvin sighed.

"Maybe it won't with your help. With all your experience, I'm sure you could be a great help to us." Lenard smiled.

He snickered, "Trust me pal, I'm no help to anyone."

"I thought the same before. Hell…sometimes I still feel that way. That's what people are for, they help," Lenard claimed.

He nodded slightly as he shifted his arm holding the bottle to Lenard, "Try some."

Lenard glanced down at the bottle, then he cautiously raised his hand and grasped onto the body of it. Marvin released it. The full weight of it fell onto Lenard's fingers. It felt uneven, some sort of liquid inside.

He raised the bottle to his lips. The unknown liquid entered his mouth. The taste was bitter, but flavorful. It radiated on his taste buds as he swallowed it. A burning sensation plagued his throat. He coughed the same as he did with the cig.

Marvin chuckled, "Damn…you really need to learn how to hold these things down." His laugh faded as Lenard's cough did, then he sighed, "Look…I'll come with you on one condition," He raised his index finger. "I'll stay for some time, to get you folks situated. But I am not staying. And you never…ever venture out to the outer woods. No matter how desperate things get, do not go there."

"I could live with that."

Marvin raised his hand to Lenard, his palm laid flat and straight. "Shake my hand." Lenard reached his hand. They clasped together as Marvin shook them in an up and down motion.

Marvin stood from the log, "Before we go, there's one thing I want to give to you." He walked to the back of the tent. He knelt down out of sight as Lenard could hear rummaging. There were clanks of metal and wood.

Marvin knelt back up with a long thin object in his hand. He held it with two hands, one at each end. He approached Lenard with this object and laid it flat on his hands in front of him.

Lenard grabbed the middle of it. The first half was a smooth line of metal painted black. The smaller half of it, divided by a circular cross guard, was wrapped in rope, with a diamond shaped pattern running down to the end.

He recognized that it was a sword of some kind. He wondered why then it did not have a blade. Marvin raised his forearm and placed his finger on the metal portion.

"It's a cover, you have to slide it off." Lenard nodded as he pushed against the metal cover.

It slowly slid off, revealing a shiny silver blade underneath. He managed to remove the cover. The blade was thin with a small curve. It was light, and the handle was firm yet comfortable to grasp onto. He raised the blade and pointed it upwards. Marvin slightly stepped back as he did.

"Woah, careful there. Those blades are dangerous. They're so sharp that even a lack-luster thrust can cut flesh deep. They're called katanas. You've used a sword before in the past, correct?" Lenard gave him a nod. "This isn't too different. Like I said, just be careful. And keep it in its cover when you aren't using it."

He aligned the blade with the slit in the cover and slid it back within. A clasping sound was made when the cross guard met the cover.

Marvin half-smiled, "That should keep you safe from any monsters."

"Thanks, I appreciate it," Lenard said as he smiled back. Marvin waved his hand. Lenard slid the cover of the blade down his belt until the hilt rested on it.

Marvin walked back to his camp to collect materials for the journey. Lenard approached the sisters and picked the torch up as he did. "What's the wait for?" Jean asked.

"Marvin's coming with us," he said.

Jean gasped as her eyes sparkled and a smile formed on her mouth. "I hope he tells me more about the outer woods on our way back. I still have so many questions."

"Try not to overload the guy, will you? We don't want him regretting this decision." Alice sighed.

Jean waved her hand, "I'm not going to ask him *too* much. I just have a couple of questions."

"Well make sure to ask them quietly. Or I might make you shut up before he does," Lenard said with a smirk. Jean glared at him as Alice laughed.

Marvin's footsteps approached them. Lenard turned to face him. A massive bag dipped down his shoulders. Tools like a shovel and the musket hung on the sides. "Jeez, what are you packing for…the end of the world."

"This trip is going to take me several weeks, not to mention the time to travel back. I need to make sure I am fully prepared," Marvin scoffed.

"Right…I guess we should get moving then." Marvin and the sisters nodded. Lenard took the lead ahead of them, following the same pebble path they took when they got there.

Crackling from the fire of the torch in Hamon's hand flowed into ear. Even though the torch allowed the two of them to talk amongst themselves, they remained silent.

He only focused on the pebble path ahead of him. There was still no sign of Lenard or the end of his pebble path as it still extended as far as the eye could see. He had lost track of how much time had passed since they last woke. He wagered it was around six hours ago. A time that could be overstated just as easily as it could be understated.

The journey had made him feel numb. His mind was only half present. Up head, now within his gaze was a bead of fire. It veered slightly to the side of the pebble path.

"Let's take a breather once we get to that fire," He said. Amber did not respond. A small campsite with one tent, two chests and a fire.

The tent was ripped open on its side. The chests were battered and flipped over with their contents spilling onto the dirt.

He sat opposite the tent in a spot not littered with MREs and water flasks. He dug the torch into the ground. The moment he sat his eyelids felt like anvils. A three day journey would not typically dock him so much.

However, he had been traveling for multiple hours on end which was not typical of an expedition. Amber sat next to him. The slight thud she made when she sat woke him a bit.

He glanced at her. The fire in front of her kept her gaze. She was trying to hide it, but she was easily as exhausted as he was. Deep eyebags and an active struggle to keep her eyes open made it easy to notice. "Let's take a good break and get some sleep."

Amber sneered as she turned her head toward him, "We slept only a couple hours ago."

"We slept over a dozen hours ago. We took a small break then. We cannot overexert ourselves," he repeated.

She groaned but did not argue and turned her eyes back to the fire. His eyebrows pinched, he then sighed.

He heard the noise of Amber's hands clapping together. He glanced and noticed she was about to pray. Hamon closed his eyes and followed the same motion as she did. A little practice they had begun engaging in together every night of this journey.

He gave the prayer in his head then opened his eyes once he finished and peeked at Amber once more. Her sight was firmly placed on the fire.

"Hey…so, we passed our deadline." Far past it in fact, Hamon thought. They were supposed to be out searching for a day and a half. Then spend the rest of the three days journeying back.

Even though they did not discuss it, he had a suspicion Amber did not plan to turn back. He did not blame her, as even he felt similar. He knew Lenard would do the same for him. "We have two options. We either head back now or…we use the supplies from the camps we come across to keep going."

"What's the catch?" Amber asked.

"The catch is exactly how it's laid out. If we keep going, we may most likely never come back to camp. Not that it's an absolute, but a good possibility," he said.

Amber nodded. Even in her current state of mind, he knew she was struggling to pick an option. He had been struggling to pick an option himself. The campsite was the only place he knew comfort. An oasis that allowed him to escape from the horrors of the forest and depravities of man, if even for a brief moment.

To have the possibility to never see that place again, even if it has been compromised, felt like a choice too unfair to bear. Not even considering the fact that the group will most certainly come searching for the two of them. Members who will search as desperately for them as they are for Lenard and the sisters.

However, they were still out there. They could be in danger, dying even. An improbable but possible chance that their only hope could be him finding them. In a way…he felt it as a sort of childish redemption for Kaylee.

A friend…no, family that he could not be quick enough to save. He was the one who allowed Kaylee to come, and he was the one who encouraged Lenard to venture out. He felt he had no right to refuse searching for him and by extension the sisters.

To refuse to continue the search would be the same as refusing to correct his own mistake. Something that he could not live the rest of his life without waking up every morning feeling crippling guilt about.

"Let's keep going," Amber answered. Their conversation has silenced for so long Hamon twitched when she spoke.

"Are you certain?" He asked her.

Her face turned uncertain. "Let's not choose one option over the other. We'll just keep going until we find Lenard and the sisters, then we'll head back. Let's not worry about whether we'll make it back or not." Hamon nodded. A decision a bit delusionary, but a necessary one if they were to continue.

"Like I said though. Let's get some rest before we head out, we can't find them if we're too tired to even spot them." Hamon smiled, Amber did so right after.

He released the straps of his bag from his shoulders and leaned back placing the full weight of his head on his bag. Amber stood up and walked out of Hamon's view. He closed his eyes as he heard shuffling from the tent.

The comfort of fabric was something she needed to sleep far more than Hamon did. He closed his eyes. He felt his body grow weightless as his mind began to dream. Worries began plaguing his mind as he drifted off.

The darkness of his vision made it easy to fall into the thoughts of his head. Then, a twig snapped. An unassuming noise. Far more quiet than the crackling of the bonfire and torch. It was subtle, but unusual. Hamon's eyes opened as he quickly turned his head toward the noise.

Two white dots peered through the darkness. He knew both him and Amber sleeping at the same time was a risk. The fire should have been more than enough to scare off any monsters. He bolted upward and grabbed the dagger hanging on the side of his bag as he did so. It laid still. Hamon held the dagger toward the monster.

He knelt to retrieve the torch and kept his eyes firmly on the creature as he did so. A black-furred, massive, clawed arm reached toward him. Hamon pointed the top of the torch at the monster.

Then, another arm came into view of the fire's light. Another arm on the monster's left, as opposed to the other. He felt a spike of panic. Monsters have four limbs, two hind legs and two front legs that functioned as arms as well.

It shouldn't be possible for a monster to reach its arms out like this without losing its balance. A deep growl came from the monster. It must not be a typical monster, somewhat like the monster that used a human body as a decoy to lure people. Shrouded in darkness must be extra limbs.

The monster right hand swiped at Hamon. He ducked down while keeping his dagger raised in the air. It slashed through the wrist of the monster. Blood splattered over Hamon's cheeks, forehead, neck and chest.

The monster screeched in pain. A screech not too dissimilar to metal scraping against metal. It towered upwards and revealed the two extra limbs Hamon had expected. Two extra front limbs connected to the monster's body just under the armpits. It raised its left arm. Hamon rolled out its range as it smashed to the ground.

"Hamon!" Amber screamed, only now seeing the monster. It turned its gaze toward her. Hamon used its distraction to slice its stomach. Its two right arms swiped at Hamon.

He dashed out of the way, but his chest still received a large but shallow cut. The weight of the monster's arms threw off its balance. He used it as an opportunity to dash back at it, then thrusted the creature's now exposed stomach with the torch and stabbed the monster with such force that it stayed firmly planted within its guts.

The screeches continued. The monster desperately clawed at its sliced stomach, furthering its own injury.

The monster fell over in pain. Hamon grasped his dagger with two hands and raised it above his head. He struck the monster on its head. Its screeches grew louder, then began to fade as its limbs grew limp.

Dark green blood poured out from under the monster and formed a puddle. Hamon tugged the dagger out of the creature's head. He stumbled backwards, almost tumbling to his feet.

Amber appeared in his view. She grasped onto his shoulders which helped him to stand upright. Beads of water rested on her eyes. He knelt into her and placed his full weight on top of her.

She nearly dropped him but managed to keep him standing up. She led him to a tree and sat him down.

"A-are you okay? Are you h-hurt anywhere?" Hamon raised his hand to the shallow cut on his chest.

She nodded, "A-any where else?" Hamon shook his head. He was just exhausted. Not even the rush of the fight made his sleepiness disappear.

"I-I'm going to get s-some supplies." She took a deep breath. "Stay here." She stood up and jogged to the tent. Hamon's vision fell too blurry to clearly see what she was doing. All he could see was her fuzzy silhouette crouching down.

He turned his head to his left, where the monster's corpse laid. The puddle of blood kept spreading. Skin bubbles formed on its back from the torch still burning within its intestines.

They began popping which caused a vomit inducing noise, and smell most likely as well. The pops, along with the splatter of melted flesh. Another unusual monster. He was unsure of what to think of it. He couldn't help but feel an overwhelming amount of dread.

Chapter 15

Noise Maker

Flowing water streamed down the wooden structure. A project hard working people came together to make. As much as Mark wanted to enjoy it, he couldn't because those five were missing. A sense of dread had plagued him. The consideration he felt of their survival had been driven dreadfully low.

Mark, Klyde and Quinton had been venturing out a couple miles here and there to look for them. However, no signs of where they went were found. No footsteps, not even any pebble paths. Which was strange to Mark, as he could have sworn he was a pebble path leading out from the far edge of the camp.

Nothing of that pebble path seems to exist anymore. Not even any dents left in the grass or dirt. It was almost as if they had completely vanished. The one piece of evidence they had to go on was Klyde's anecdote that Amber was talking with him.

Mark stood at the wall of the artificial river. Picc was on the other side and prepared the water mill. Mark kept his eyes on the flowing water. The sound of wood and nails being hammered, along with the noise of flowing water invaded his head. Jarold was over to the side of the structure. Jarold and him watched it to ensure no water was leaking from the rubber tubes.

The hammering stopped, “It’s done!” Picc shouted. Mark raised his head to him. He stood a couple feet away from it with his hands placed on his hips.

Mark walked around the structure and met Picc on the other side. The mill was a circle with wooden planks protruding out evenly across it. It stood three feet tall and had a metal protrusion on the right side.

“Help me haul it,” He said as he twitched his head in the direction of the structure. Mark nodded and grabbed the mill by the circular metal poles that outlined the planks.

Picc grabbed the other side. They lifted it together. It was lighter than its size and they were able to carry it to the structure where they placed it within. The metal protrusion on its side clasped onto the wooden walls of the river.

The water pushed on the planks that were now in contact. It was slow to move at first. It then began to pick up speed. The planks stagnated at a speed fast enough to make it hard to follow them with the eyes.

“Look at that.” Picc grinned from ear to ear. A marvelous creation unlike anything Mark had seen before. Its glory could only do so much to quench the dread he felt at that moment. In the back of his mind all he could think about was the safety of his missing group members. Lost out in the woods.

Lenard had his left hand grasped onto the handle of his new katana. His other hand carried the torch. He kept an eye peeled as he wanted to be ready for a monster to attack them at any moment.

They used the compass to travel north-east. The direction Marvin suspected their camp was. Three days of traveling had passed so far. Behind him the sisters were with Marvin. Jean had been hounding him with various questions. Alice had been attempting to get her to stop.

"So…what are some other cool stuff your old group did?" Jean asked.

"Our population was large enough that we made teams of people to venture out for different materials. We had a food team, water team, clothing team, tools team and outer woods team," Marvin said.

"That sounds awesome! Were you a part of the outer woods team?" Marvin nodded. "Who else?" Jean questioned.

"We had our captain, his name was Isaac. There was another fellow named Alan. We had one more member, Matthew. He didn't join us until later, he was a timid fellow," Marvin listed each of the members with a finger.

So the black-haired man is Alan, and the timid one is Matthew, Lenard thought while he recounted his dream sequence. There is still a lot that doesn't make sense, even with Marvin's explanation of the outer woods.

What was that breathing? Another creature. That didn't seem so. Also, Lenard knew for a fact he was not out in the outer woods when he was in isolation. He sighed as he rubbed the back of his head with his left hand.

Marvin appeared next to him, "Something wrong, good friend?"

Lenard wiped his eye bags, "No…hey, did you ever hear breathing from above? Like, when you were in the outer woods and all that."

Marvin shook his head, "No sir. I'm curious to hear what you're talking about."

No lead on that. Lenard sneered. His noticeable frustration made Marvin's gaze grow more curious. "When I was on my own. There was a moment I remember. Silence, then a faint breathing sound coming from above me," Lenard said.

Marvin leaned his head back and placed his hand on his chin, "Are you certain that you weren't dreaming? I've never heard anything like that from anyone before."

Lenard shrugged his left shoulder and made a frustrated sigh as he did so. "I'm not too sure. It felt way too vivid to be one. I can't remember it now, but I do know there was never a moment after that where I could have woken up."

"Hmm," Marvin swiped his thumb against his bottom lip. "And you're positive that you weren't in the outer woods?" Lenard nodded. He shrugged, "I have got nothin,' good friend."

Lenard's body slumped. There was still more he had to figure out. Like who was the blurry face individual. The amount of unknowns was getting to him. He breathed in deeply, then exhaled and cleared his mind to help stay focused on getting back home.

Amber kept herself close to Hamon. He had been fine for the most part, with a bandage that now covered the cut on his chest. Every so often she would ask him if there is any pain, or if the bandage is loose.

Both were not, but Hamon doubted he would tell her even if they were. Amber couldn't help but stay worried about him.

It took him ages to get proper rest after the attack. They were back traveling along the path now.

He had to reassure her multiple times that he could keep going. She was still somewhat unconvinced that he was uninjured aside from his chest.

They had lost track of time. It could have been anywhere between a week to twelve days. The uncertainty had picked away at them and slowly deteriorated their psyche.

The endless pebble path was doing that to them as well. At this point, both of them knew that there was no possible way Lenard and the sisters were out this far. They could not have had this many pebbles on them.

They could collect the various pebbles scattered throughout the woods, but that alone would not be enough to create a path this long. And yet, they continued. Driven by some force that told them to keep going. As well as the pebble path being their one lead on them.

Something must have happened. His mind had been too numb to speculate. It's not like speculation would do him any good anyways. Either way, he clinged to hope. He could not let shewing off Lenard and ignoring his concerns be the last time the two would talk.

The idea of last meetings plagued his mind in general. There was a powerful sense of dread that he knew they both felt. Even if they were to turn back now, there is only a small chance they could make it back.

The further they continued the more they cemented their fate. Walking down a pebble path to their deaths. Even if they haven't been on good terms, he knew that she could not have been happy with never seeing Klyde again. He felt a tinge of guilt. He was the one who brought her along. Who begged her for her help. Now she will most likely die again. Isolated. Away from the ones she loves.

Hamon attempted to keep his thoughts clear of these thoughts by focusing on the colors and shapes of the pebbles in front of them.

Some were gray, others were a pale red. The distance between the pebbles ranged from a couple of inches to several feet. The pebbles formed a nearly perfect straight line.

All of this was typical for pebble laying. Even if these pebbles were not placed by Lenard or one of the sisters, it was placed by *someone*. That very little difference gave him a small boost in motivation. He wondered if Amber noticed it as well.

Most likely not, as she did not share the same experience with venturing as Hamon did. He thought of telling her. To at least give her something to cling onto.

"Hey," She said just as Hamon had finished his thought. "Are your bandages still on tight?" Her routine checkup.

"Yeah…uhh…I think. Judging by these pebbles. Whoever's trail we're on, it's at least a person." A bit out of nowhere. He realized it when he said it.

"Okay. Do you not think it could be Lenard's?" A strange question. He reformulated his thoughts within his head in an effort to answer her.

"I…I'm not sure. If it is, then something supernatural is happening." He hoped that would be enough to answer her question without making her feel less motivated.

She remained quiet. He assumed that meant she was done asking questions. Another dose of guilt troubled him. He couldn't help but interpret her silence as a worsening sense of faith. The shame haunted him enough to cause him to turn his head in a knee-jerk reaction.

He then gazed to the side and saw something just on the edge of the torch's light. Something strange. He halted in his tracks. Amber's footsteps paused as well.

It was a black object that was nearly invisible to the eye. The light from the torch reflecting off of it was the only thing that made it detectable.

"What is it?" She asked.

"I don't know," He said. The light mirrored onto the object into distorted lines of orange. He stepped toward it and approached it. It was large. Too heavy to haul around anywhere.

Casings of silver and black overlapped each other in strange ways. Two circle shaped objects rested on the front and back of it. A leather mat was placed on its center. A black metal casing dug into it, on the other end it led to a pair of handles that protruded from the sides.

On its front was two glass casings, containing bulbs that looked similar to the one from Picc's sketches of the flashlight. White paint made lined patterns. The object itself was unnaturally smooth for something in *the forest*. The circles looked familiar. He knelt down to review it. They were made from rubber, the same as the tubes they made. But why? What was this object and why was it out here?

He stood up, "Let's get going." Amber followed him back to the pebble path where they continued forward. The object eventually faded into complete darkness.

Lenard found himself in another dream sequence. He was conscious enough to be aware of that much, unlike the other times. This time he was laying in a tent covered in soft blankets that felt too good to get out of. He spent more time there than he would like to admit.

He got himself out of the covers, unzipped the tent and crawled out. Not many people were out. The first thing he noticed. The second was the true size of the camp.

The fuzziness he felt before obscured his view of it. That fuzziness was gone now, and the complete scope of the campsite was now his to lay eyes on. Marvin did not lie when he described it as a utopia. There were several campfires, each one with two or more tents surrounding it.

Based on the number of tents, he realized his initial estimate of a population of twenty was wrong. There had to be thirty…no forty people living here. Over quadruple the size of his own camp.

Then he remembered the man with the blurry face. He gazed across the camp and saw one man at the fire his tent was next to. The man sat on a log and was facing to the right of him. It was Marvin. The blonde hair was enough for him to recognize him. He stood up and walked to him.

Marvin noticed him as he approached, “Sleep well, Picc?” Lenard’s eyes widened, then remembered who he was in these dream sequences. He took his seat next to him as he nodded.

“How about you?” Now that he could see more clearly, he noticed just how young Marvin looked in these dreams then he did now. He had no beard, his hair was soft and there was far less wrinkles on his face.

His general face made him appear to be in his early twenties. Nothing like the present, where he looked to be late forties, possibly even early fifties. This meant the dream sequences must be seeing into the past. Something he had already suspected, but now was confirmed.

"I haven't gotten the chance," he laughed. "The captain's been working us to the bone. He's been making us log all the different creatures we've come across." A log? Why wouldn't Marvin have mentioned that to them? Maybe because it wasn't useful to their current situation?

"You wouldn't mind showing that to me? Would you?" He asked.

Marvin shook his head, "Sorry, the captain wants only I and Alan to have eyes on it. Been referring to it by that term you taught us…what was it?"

"Confidentiality." He had no idea how he even knew the term, no less its definition. Another bit of information that suddenly entered his brain, like someone put it there. Marvin nodded his head as he bounced his index finger at him.

"That's the word. So, sorry about that. I would tell you if I could." A dead end in that department. He wondered why that was bothering him so much. Never before did he care about having knowledge on something.

"Don't worry about it, good friend." A phrase he didn't even mean to utter. He had heard it so much from Marvin that he said it on instinct.

Marvin raised his eyebrow as he half-smiled, "I've never been called that before. I like it. Mind if I borrow it?" Lenard nodded his head slightly.

That whole exchange he found to be weird. The thought that he might have been the one to get Marvin in the habit of saying that made him feel strange. It made the dream sequence feel more like time-travel.

Another idea came across his mind. “Hey, did you ever experience or come across a monster that made breathing from above?” A question he had already asked, but maybe he could get another answer here.

Marvin furrowed his brow. He anticipated what the answer would be from that action. “I haven’t…but now that you’ve mentioned it. There was someone who claimed they did.” He felt bewildered but satisfied. Marvin had lied to him. However, he was now getting some answers.

“Matthew, you’d have to ask him. He’s blind, but can hear a pebble drop twenty feet away. He said something about that back when he was with his old group,” Marvin said.

Matthew, he wasn’t sure what blind meant, but he knew he experienced the same as him, and if he talked to him then he could find signs that could bring him closer to an answer.

He smiled, “Where can I talk to him?” Marvin pointed off into the far distance. Over a hundred feet away, at another bonfire was a man sitting on his own. He could only make out his basic silhouette from such a distance. He stood up, turned to Marvin, grasped his hand and shook it. “Thank you.”

Marvin’s gaze magnified. “No problem…good friend.” He turned back away from hand and strolled toward Matthew. “Try not to overwhelm the guy! He’s real sensitive!” Lenard lifted his arm and raised his thumb in view of Marvin.

Once he was closer more details of Matthew became clear to him. He had the same bright-brown, curly hair he remembered. Like before, he had his hands clasped together in the center of his lap.

His eyes faced toward the fire and his entire body gesture was tucked in. He appeared to be a sensitive man indeed. Matthew had noticed him approaching. His gaze rested onto him but wasn't aligned.

Almost as if he didn't know where quite to look. When he got close enough to notice even smaller details, that's when he noticed his eyes. They were completely shaded. A sight that made him feel a prick of anxiety.

"Who's there?" Matthew asked.

He raised his forearms. "It's just me." Next to the man was a stick, one resting on an angle against the log. It was carved. "What's the stick for?"

Matthew grasped onto the stick, as if he were worried he might try to take it from him. He sat on the log to the right of the man. "It's my eyes."

Lenard furrowed his brow, "Your eyes? The hell does that mean?" The man's eyes did not land on him as they spoke. He grew curious as to why.

"It's how I see. I can't see like you or other people do. My normal eyes don't work." His voice was shallow and high pitched, yet relaxed. Not at all what he had expected given his posture.

"You can't see? Not at all? That sounds like a pain in the ass," Lenard said.

Matthew nodded as he smiled, "Sometimes it is, but the way you guys describe *the forest*, doesn't sound like there's a whole lot to see anyway." Lenard gave a good belly laugh, then placed the palm of his hand on his stomach.

"You got that right, good friend," He said again on instinct. He hoped it would not be a cat name he would pick up himself. "My name's…" He hesitated for a moment, almost saying his real name. "It's Picc. I came to talk with you because I heard some rumors that you experienced the sound of breathing from above."

He bowed his head. He grasped onto his eyes using both hands and stood up. "I heard it straight from above. Clear as glass. A faint, raspy breathing noise." Lenard smiled as he scooched himself closer to the man. Someone who finally shared his experience.

"Well, I'm coming to talk to you about this because I heard the same thing," Lenard claimed.

Matthew's mouth gaped, then slowly formed into a smile, "Really?! I thought I was the only one. No one would believe me." Matthew shifted his weight back and forth against the stick. Lenard raised his palms.

"I'm as happy as you are." He did not lie as he understood the excitement that radiated from him. "But I need to hear more about it. Do you remember anything about that breathing noise?"

Matthew placed his hand on his chin, "Like I said, it was faint and raspy. Like it was someone breathing with a bad cough. But…It also didn't sound human at the same time. It only sounded *like* it was human." All things Lenard knew well. Memories of it clawed back into his brain of the event.

"What else?" He asked.

"Hmm…Well, when it slowly went away, the way the sound was moving was really strange. When the sound was moving away, it went further, but kept in the same place in the air. It also sounded like it was really far up." That's exactly what he was looking for. He smiled from ear to ear in satisfaction.

With this, he could propose a couple of theories. Maybe it was some sort of flying monster? It could be the thing Marvin suspected of leading *The Nothingness* to them. That wouldn't make sense however, as that means Marvin had to have heard the breathing from above at some point. He could be lying, or it could need to be very quiet in order to hear the noise.

"Where were you when you heard it?" He asked.

"I was on a mission to the outer woods with the guys. They didn't believe me when I said I heard it," Matthew said. Lenard nodded, "I know you said it was faint? But was it quiet? The breathing, I mean." Back when he experienced it, the breathing was audible, enough to be impossible to not hear.

Matthew rattled his head, "No sir. I was shocked when the others said they didn't hear anything. Even when they were making a bunch of noise, I still heard it."

That removes that possibility. Something else then? Marvin said Matthew has really good hearing, could that be it? It frustrated him. Even with the perspective he was dying to get, it answered almost nothing.

He spiked his lip and looked down as he clenched his fists. "There is one more thing I would like to say." He glared at him. "The breathing. I found it strange…because I swore I could hear it coming from multiple places."

Chapter 16

Liar

Lenard awoke to a hand shaking his shoulder. His eyes opened as a silhouette of a person came into focus.

"Wake up," Alice said. He shewed her hand away using the back palm. He squinted his eyes. Alice was crouched in front of him. He leaned his head upright, off a bit further in the distance Jean and Marvin stood. They looked down at him with their hands leaned on the straps of their bags.

He realized they were prepared to leave. He leaned up and stood upward as he sighed. He could hear Alice giggle at his apparent sleepiness.

His bag laid at his feet and his back ached as he reached down and grabbed it. The straps were flung around his shoulders.

"Glad to have you back from the dead," Jean teased as she wore a mischievous smile. He sneered as he glared at her.

Alice snickered behind him before she rejoined her sister. Marvin now had a hold of the torch. The two stared at each other before Lenard turned his sight away. He did not know how to feel about him after he learned that he had lied.

Perhaps he might have been too harsh. After all, the things he lied about were not too extreme. It could be that he lied in order to stop him from exploring the outer woods.

"Are you ready to go?" Marvin asked. He twitched as he was distracted from his own thoughts. He nodded. "Then let's get moving." Marvin turned around toward the dark opening made from the trees.

The sisters followed Marvin first, he ensued right after. The light of the camp they rested at seeped off his skin. A restless void awaited them.

Klyde sat at a rock half-way buried into the ground with his back palms on his forehead and his elbows on his knees. Mark knew the frustration well. It was only moments before when he was sitting with the exact posture. He could somewhat relate to the pain of losing one's wife. Alice, someone he had grown close to, could also be dead.

Not even imagination could bring him close to understanding Klyde's suffering. Another camp they explored with no sign of their missing members. This camp was further out…much further out. Two tents, with supplies littered everywhere, but they did not intend to take anything.

They did not carry enough bags to do so even if they had wished to. It had been almost a month since they had gone missing. The idea that they all had met their untimely ends was now realized by them. The most devastating loss they've had. Over half their group could possibly be dead.

All he could feel was overwhelming dread. Five members missing will take them years to recover from, if they recover at all.

This was the first group he had ever been with. He had resided with them for as long as he could remember. The tragic stories he had heard about the more experienced members losing their groups was something he began thinking about plenty. With the way things were, he felt as if those tragedies were becoming reality before his eyes. Klyde stood up and sighed.

"Let's head back," He whispered. Klyde's gaze stood firm on the bonfire in front of him. Mark clenched his fists and bit his lip.

"Are you sure? We can look around a bit more." An offer to Klyde, but it was more for his sake. He did not want to let go of the hope that they could still be alive. That they could stumble across something that will give them an actual lead.

"No…we've been out here too long. Besides, we should help Picc finish the flashlight." Mark furrowed his brow. Why was he still focused on that? It was Klyde's marriage, something he had no real say in. However, he felt as if Klyde should be more concerned about this. As if his level of panic was quite right. "Once it's finished, we should be able to find them much more easily, no?" Klyde grinned.

He smiled. Perhaps he was wrong. Maybe Klyde is just far more levelheaded than he is. He had been the more of the emotional type after all. Besides, now was no time to speculate amongst one another.

Klyde walked past him and followed the pebble path behind him. He turned around as he passed and followed him. There was one topic he was still curious about.

He approached Klye's side, "Do you know why Hamon and Amber went off together to find them?"

Klyde sighed, "It was my fault. I told him not to be concerned about them. I think the way I brushed him off made him feel like he was on his own. I would have joined him if I knew he was this desperate to find them."

He sneered. Something didn't feel quite right, "Then why just those two? Why didn't he let me, Jarold or Quinton come with?" It was right of him to think that didn't make sense.

All three of them had more experience venturing than Amber did. Even having an extra member with them would be much more beneficial. He scooched out of the way of a tree in his path.

"I think he didn't trust Picc. I don't know why. Something about him just rubbed him the wrong way I guess. I think us siding with Picc over him made him feel he was up against us, like he could trust us. He must have trusted Amber since she wasn't on Picc's side either. That's my theory on it anyway."

That still didn't sound right. Even if Hamon didn't trust him, he was sensible enough to at least discuss this with him. Something must have pushed him away. A sense he maybe had felt from Klyde, not Picc. Maybe Hamon knew something he did not, about Klyde or Picc. An idea formed in his head.

"You don't think they snuck off together to…you know," Mark implied.

Klyde gave him a blank stare, "No."

He shrugged, "Just an idea. You could never know for sure." Then why? Why would those two run off together with no one else? There had to be a deeper reason as to why. That doesn't even answer the question of how they went missing.

Their intent was to bring Lenard and the sisters back. Then why would they not leave a pebble path? Surely they would want to return home. Could Klyde or Picc be untrustworthy enough to want to cut all of them off completely. That couldn't be it. Hamon was reasonable and kind, he's not the type of man who'd abandon everyone because of a suspicion.

He couldn't form a good reason in his head why there was no pebble path. But…what if…someone got rid of it? But who could move so many pebbles so quickly?

"Are you okay?" Klyde asked.

He twitched as he turned his head to face him, "Uhh…yeah. Yeah, I'm fine. You know, it's just that this whole thing has me overthinking. You know?"

Klyde smiled as he nodded his head, "I know what you mean. Trust me, we're all concerned about their safety."

What Klyde said. It almost made him crease his eyebrows on instinct. It was the way Klyde said it. When he was young, Klyde would tell him lies about his parents. He was told that they passed on peacefully from old age, but he caught on to what really happened.

In this world, no one dies peacefully and from old age. What happens is you get old enough to be too much of a liability. Then, left behind. He was sure that was the fate of his parents and learned quickly of what Klyde's lying voice sounded like. The way Klyde said it. Why did it sound like a lie?

Lenard swore he could see something move in the corner of his eye. A black mass in the distance. It disappeared when he laid his eyes on it. He questioned whether or not what he saw was real. The sudden turn of his head caught Marvin's attention. "What's wrong?"

"Nothing," He whispered under his breath as he shifted his head back. Marvin wore a suspicious glare. According to him, they were at the center of the inhabited woods. It had taken them two weeks to get there.

He could tell the journey was taking its toll on the sisters. Their constant bickering had grown silent now. Sometimes when he would look back at them to check up, he would see Jean leaning on her sister's shoulder. A sign of compassion that gave him that little push he needed to keep going.

As well as the questions he still had in his head. As much as he used to mock Hamon for it, having a goal to focus on made him feel more motivated. Like he has something to strive toward and accomplish.

It had been as desirable as it was frustrating. The lack of answers and how impossible they felt to get made sure of that. He had not had another dream sequence since the one where he talked to Matthew.

These dream sequences were very inconsistent. When he was on the grand expedition, in only a couple days he experienced two dream sequences. Despite twice the amount of time passing on this journey, he had only had one. It's erraticness made him irritated to no end. He wished he could just know already what triggers it.

If he did, he could have a lot more answers. In the meantime, he wanted to piece together a chronological order of these dream sequences. He no longer believed them to follow the pattern he had originally suspected. In total, he had four dream sequences. The first one had to be the last one. If that was truly from Picc's point of view, then he must have answers on the *breathing from above*, since he must have heard it. He hadn't asked Picc about it, so the possibility was certainly there.

But Marvin was there as well, could he also be lying about it? Marvin in the dream sequence had said he had no knowledge of it, but maybe that was before the first dream sequence. That meant the fourth one had been before the first one.

As for the other two, there was no possible way to place them anywhere. He had no sense of when those took place. Maybe some careful questioning could change that, he thought as he shifted his gaze to Marvin. "Hey, I never asked you how you really knew Picc. I'm curious to know."

Marvin smirked as he kept his eyes forward, "Well, since he knew things about the other world, he would come on outer woods expeditions with us. When we would come across objects from the other world there, he would give us mini lessons on it. None of us paid much attention to it though." He laughed, "Although the captain would yell at us if we didn't mark it down. He was the only one who was obsessed with the other world…other than Picc himself of course."

Another log? That will be useful for his next dream sequence. There's no reason why the list he contributed to would be hidden from him like the monster log. Then he had a sort of realization. He had been accusing Marvin in his head of being untruthful and hidden, when he was doing the exact same thing.

A thought that made him feel a bit guilty for how he treated him. "So…Picc was a friend of yours, I guess."

Marvin nodded as his smile morphed into more of a half-smile. "I was the only one who bonded with him. I was more interested in the other world itself than what remnants of it lied here. That wouldn't stop him from telling me about it.

There was one thing I remember. He claimed he had memories of his mother from the other world."

His eyes widened. To Marvin, it was a natural reaction. He had worn that gaze for a different reason. That story was one he told to Marvin in the dream sequence. This confirmed his suspicion of the dreams being connected to reality.

"I know, it sounds pretty exciting. I wish I got to know more…but he didn't remember anything else," Marvin shrugged. The dream sequences were like time travel. They were bringing him to previous points in time. "How's he doing anyway?"

"Oh…uhh, fine. He certainly seems to be in high spirits. There's something I'm confused about." When they first came across Marvin, he stated that he did not trust them because of a past experience with someone else. "Who was it you said betrayed you?"

Marvin sneered, "My old captain. He was a bastard. He would stockpile information about the outer woods and only share a portion of it with us. A buddy of mine, Alan, died that way, getting attacked by a monster that was logged but not shown to us." The log! That was his key. If he could see that, maybe there will be more information on the *breathing from above*.

He placed the tips of his fingers on Marvon's arm, "Do you still have that log?" Marvin raised an eyebrow. He pursed his lips as he did not realize how suspicious that sounded. Marvin shook his head.

"Sorry, good friend. The captain kept it in his hut. It was left behind when our camp was attacked. I would have brought it with me had I known how valuable it could have been," Marvin said.

No luck now, but there was still the dream sequence. If he could enter one again, then he can get ahold of that log. The only problem was slipping into a dream sequence. With no way to trigger it, there was no way to tell if he would ever enter another dream sequence again.

Then, *something* heard his wish. The crackling of Marvin's torch stopped. Lenard glanced over in his direction only for him to be gone. The illumination from the torch still hovered in the air, even with no fire to generate it. He turned. The sisters were gone as well. The panic he felt began to calm itself. Not at his command. Almost as if he were being forced to calm down. His eyes grew tired and he fell to the ground.

When they arrived back to camp, the little hope Klyde had given Mark had all but vanished. The sight of the camp made him feel a wave of depression. The amount of tents now outnumbered the number of remaining members. Both Jarold and Quinton sat with slumped postures.

The fires seemed dimmer somehow. As if light itself has grown darker. The only one who was not affected was Picc. He couldn't lie and say that he didn't feel a sense of anger at how little the situation had troubled him.

He knew better than to explore that sense of spite. Picc has only been a member of theirs for a couple of months. It would not be fair to say he should experience the same level of pain as they do when he does not know them. Picc was messing with the artificial river, on the side where Klyde and him were approaching. When Picc heard their footsteps, he turned to see them. He greeted them with a large grin. “Find anything?”

Klyde and Mark stopped a couple feet away from him. “Nothing. I figured it would be better to wait for your flashlight to be built before we look again.” Picc closed his eyes as raised his eyebrows and pursed his lips.

“That’s too bad. But maybe it’s time to give up the search. It’s highly unlikely that any of them are alive. Even if they are, we’ll still probably never see them again.” Mark sneered. That was a horrible idea, he thought. Although they did not have much to work with, their missing members are family, they could not give up looking for them.

“Give us one more try. With the flashlight. If we find nothing, then we’ll move on.” He fixed his glare on Klyde.

“What the hell are you talking about? We can’t stop looking for them!” He gestured his arm toward *the forest* behind them.

“We can’t go looking forever. We’ll never recover as a group if we do so. It’s what needs to be done,” Klyde said while he kept his gaze on Picc.

He scoffed. Klyde planned on giving up. It struck him with a sense of betrayal. He felt isolated. Like he was on his own. If Klyde gave up, he would still continue on, with or without him. He wondered if that’s how Hamon felt when Lenard and the sisters went missing. He understood why they may have left. He shifted his eyes away from the two of them and walked away toward the center fire.

Klyde did not call to him, despite his noticeable anger. That added further to his isolated state of mind. At the center bonfire, Jarold and Quinton sat around it. Jarold was sitting at the farthest end from him with his legs crossed and his right palm placed on his chin.

The force of his chin leaning on it made the flesh of his cheeks squished upwards. Across the fire was Quinton, who was also sitting, legs crossed with an MRE in his left hand. He approached him from behind and sat down next to him.

He stretched out his legs and rested both palms on the ground behind him. Quinton shifted his sight from the MRE to him. "You're back. Find anything?" He sighed as he shifted his head. "I'll take that as a no."

He groaned as he adjusted his body to balance on its own, then raised his arms and clenched his fingers. "It's so damn frustrating. I feel like I'm the only one that wants to keep looking." He did not mean to spill so much emotion. It came out naturally, almost on instinct. Quinton placed his hand on his shoulder.

"I get how you feel, but I don't think now is a great time to be getting angry at each other," Quinton said.

A fair point. He would probably feel the same way if so much time hadn't passed. Each second began to feel like a ticking time-bomb. Every second wasted would mean more time than the five members would parish.

"I know…but I just want something. Anything that will tell me that they're at least alive. I don't understand how everyone can just sit around, not doing anything and still be so calm." Quinton's palm slid from his shoulder to his back.

"We're all just as panicked as you are." Quinton retracted his arm and placed it on the spoon resting in the MRE. He scooped out a large chunk of chicken broth and ate it. The slight hum of satisfaction that came from Quinton made him feel hungry as well.

He had not eaten in quite some time as he could not find the appetite. The hours of venturing he had done with Klyde while they searched was enough to make any man starve. When Quinton brought his gaze back to him, his hunger was noticeable. Quinton smirked.

"Let me go get you something to eat. We'll discuss this more once you are properly fed." Quiton handed his MRE to him as he stood up. Mark watched as he wandered off to the food chest and took out another MRE. Hunger. Perhaps that was all it was. A good meal to clear his senses. Quinton brought the new MRE to the fire and set it up to roast above the fire. He then sat back down next to Mark, who handed him his MRE back.

"Thank you. I appreciate you getting me something to eat." Quinton smiled.

"That's no problem." Some food would do him nicely. Nonetheless, his mind could not escape the anxiety of the missing members. All he could think about is if they were well fed themselves, and hoped they were not starving.

Chapter 17

Bastard

Lenard awoke within a tent once more. This time, the fuzziness he felt entering these dream sequences had vanished. Everything was so clear it was almost indistinguishable from reality. A sensation that felt even more strange than the fuzziness itself.

He uncovered himself from the blanket on top of him and crawled out the same as before. This time, everything looked all too familiar. There were a huge amount of tents, yet a lack of people. Marvin rested at the fire nearest to him.

Everything was the same as the dream sequence from before. Why? He stood up and walked to the fire where Marvin sat. "Sleep well, Picc?" The exact same words and tone.

This wasn't another event, it was a repeat. No…it was a second chance. Whoever had been showing him these dream sequences was giving him one last opportunity to figure out the secrets. This was his last chance. Yet, there was a problem. When he entered this dream sequence, it was in the middle of traveling with Marvin and the sisters.

If there was any sort of consistency to this, that meant he was currently passed out on the ground. In the middle of *the forest.*

In order to achieve the answers he wants, he would need to stay here and put those three in danger. When there is no bonfire around, the chances of getting attacked by a monster are far more likely. He could depend on Marvin to take care of any danger that came their way.

That was his one option, he had to rely on him. He turned his back toward Marvin and gazed across the camp. Its full glory now in his view. Several dozen tents littered. Chests overflowed with materials. In the center was a structure. One distinct from the tents. It was made of wood, and much larger. The roof was constructed out of leaves.

He glanced back at Marvin, who no longer sat at the log. A hand fell onto his shoulder. His body twitched as he turned to see Marvin beside him. "Where are you going?" Marvin asked in a firm tone. His expression was blank.

"Uh…I wanted to see the item log. There's something I want to see," Lenard said.

Marvin's face softened as he smiled, "Oh, come with me then." He gestured his hand as he walked past him. He led Lenard to the front of the hut. A door blocked the entrance.

Marvin made three quiet knocks with two fingers. They waited. After a couple seconds the door opened with the captain standing at the entrance. "Captain. Picc here wanted to see the item log."

The captain's large body blocked his sight from most of the inside. He could see a lantern hanging from the ceiling and a wooden structure to the right. The captain glanced at him with an overwhelming gaze.

One hand was placed on the edge of the doorway, the other on the door itself. His clear state of mind allowed him to see just how intimidating the captain really was. "For what reason?"

Marvin glanced at him as he waited for his response. He cleared his throat and took a deep breath as he relaxed all of the muscles. His body loosened. "I was hoping to look over it. I think there might be a way to build the musket." A risk of a lie. He was unsure if they have or have not discovered the musket yet.

The captain sharpened his gaze as he shifted it to Marvin once last time. He lowered his hand from the doorway and scooched to the side. "You can look, but only for a little bit. Marvin will watch over you." Lenard and Marvin nodded. He walked inside.

Within was a wood plated floor. To the left was a bed with a wooden frame. The warm air mixed with the wood gave a distinct oak smell. On the wooden structure he saw to the right, there were papers littered across it. Some were blank, others had writing on them. Above the structure was a string with pieces of paper attached to it by clips.

On the wooden structure there were cupboards, two stacked vertically on both sides, with papers and books filled it. One of those books had to be the monster log.

The captain stepped in front of him and pulled out a book from the bottom left cupboard. He turned to Lenard and handed the book to him. The cover of the book was made from leather with pages unevenly stacked between.

The book was around three inches thick. It had an earthy mixed with inky smell. On the front cover read 'Log of All Items Discovered In The Outer Woods.' He opened the book.

Each page had a drawing of an item in the top left corner with a description filling the rest of the page. Each description contained information on what the item is called, when it was found, what its purpose was and what it was used for in the other world.

There was also a small list of uses the item had. The list included items like machetes, kites, straws, staplers, carpets, tables, desks and so much more. One Item he recognized as he was flipping through the pages were glasses. He stopped at the page and read through the description.

An item with two metal handles that rest on the ears that connect to two glass panes that sit in front of the eyes. Used in the other world to help those with stunted vision see better. Can be harvested for glass or metal. Item Rarity: Rare.

"Find anything useful?" A deep voice asked.

He glanced up to the captain, who had his arms crossed and stared at him. "Um…I…This is useful. But…Is it possible I could get a look at the monster log? I feel I will get all the info I need if I could see that." It was a lie without much planning. It could do the trick, but it will fall apart if he is questioned any further on it.

The captain sneered and unwrapped his arms. He turned toward the desk and grabbed another book from the cupboard. This book was in the top right. It was placed vertically at the end and was hidden by the papers stacked in front of it.

"You're really going to show him?" Marvin asked. The captain nodded. Lenard set the item log on the bed behind him, then raised his arms toward the captain.

The captain placed the book into his hands. The smell and make of the book was the same as the other. The only difference was the cover, instead of 'Items' it was now 'Creatures.'

He opened it. The layout was the exact same as the other log, pictures on the top left, description on the rest. Abnormal creatures splattered the pages. There were monsters that had six limbs, others had two heads. Some creatures had no similar appearance to the ones that sprung the inhabited woods.

There were tentacle, sludge and cave monsters. Then, he landed on the page he was looking for. The creature that was simply titled as *Breathing From Above.* Its drawing was the point of view of the woods when faced upwards.

Its description read: *A faint breathing noise that can be heard in uncertain conditions. The breathing noise sounds human but is not. What causes the breathing noise is unknown. If you hear this breathing noise, run. As when it occurs, monsters will usually follow. The breathing has been described as raspy or dry. From Reports, it seems the breathing may be coming from multiple points. The breathing noise itself seems to travel, and always in a straight line. It has no estimated size nor appearance.*

A spike of disappointment struck him. There was finally a description on the *breathing from above*, and yet it barely knew any more than he did. There had to be more. He flipped to the next page to see if there was a continuation.

The next page was a description of *The Nothingness.* He sighed as he was just about to close the book. His eyes landed on a line that caught his attention. 'Warning. To all those who spot this monster, DO NOT return home. It will follow you.' He respread the page.

This creature has been referred to also as *The Lurker*. When it spots a group of venturers on an expedition, it will hide in the background and follow them. Once those venturers return to camp, *The Nothingness* will then proceed to destroy the entire campsite. There is no known way to escape from *The Nothingness's* sight once it catches on to you.

His mouth gaped and his eyes spread. In a slow motion, he brought his hands together and closed the book.

Marvin noticed his expression, "Are you alright?" He shifted his gaze to him. He lied to them…that *bastard.* Marvin must have known about it, not in whatever time Lenard was now, but currently. When he was leading Lenard and the sisters home…he must have known about it. *The Nothingness* attacked Marvin's camp, he must know.

Lenard awoke by being shook with great force. He jolted upward. Beside him on each side were the sisters, who he glanced at both. Alice was to his right, Jean to his left. Both of them had tears streaming down their eyes.

Their mouths were opened, but all he heard were muffles. They lunged at him and wrapped their arms around him. The blurry hearing and sight cleared out. A dozen feet away in front of him was Marvin, who leaned against a tree with his arms crossed and one foot supporting his weight. The sister's cries became fully audible. Lenard brought his sight back to them and placed the palms of his hands on the back of their heads.

He stood up. The sisters followed his motion. "Y-you passed out again," Alice cried. He turned to her and placed both his hands on her shoulder.

"I'm…I'm fine." The sisters backed away as they began clearing the tears from their eyes. "Something's telling me that's the last time that will happen." They nodded. He returned to Marvin.

"Glad to see you're okay, good friend. But we should get moving, we saw *The Nothingness* not too far behind." Marvin's expression, his lack of concern.

He knew. Lenard sizzled with rage as he walked to Marvin and pulled out the Katana. Marvin stood up from the tree and took a step forward. He raised his hand. Lenard placed both of his hands on the metal cover then swung the handle into Marvin's face. His head rattled as he collapsed to the ground.

"You lying piece of shit!" Two pairs of arms wrapped around his shoulders and pulled him back. Marvin sat up with his hand clutching his nose. Blood poured from the nostrils as well as the gash from the blow. "You knew!! You were leading that thing right to us!" Small beads of water formed in Marvin's eyes.

"What the hell are you on about!?" Marvin asked. Lenard stopped pushing against the sisters' grips. They released him.

"You know exactly what the hell I'm talking about!" The sisters positioned themselves in front of him. Their palms raised and bodies spread to defend Marvin.

"Can we all calm down for a second! Lenard, what the hell are you doing?" Alice asked. They lowered their hands as he slid the katana back into his belt.

"You can ask him. That thing," He pointed out into the abyss above the trees, "*The Nothingness*, we didn't just see it by coincidence. It's following us, and it will do so until we reach camp. Then it will kill all of us. And he knew that! He knew that fucking thing would kill us once we got back home!" The sisters' eyes widened as they turned to face Marvin.

Marvin gritted his teeth, "It's your own damn fault. You lead that thing right to my camp! If I hadn't it would have killed me!" Lenard groaned as he re-approached him. The sisters caught him before he could reach Marvin. "How the hell do you know about that anyway! No one should have!"

The sisters pushed Lenard back and kept their hands placed on him to stop him. He pointed at Marvin, "You're going to help us fix this! You're going to get that thing away from us!"

Marvin shook his head as he stood up, "There is no stopping that thing. It will follow us to your camp, we can't shake it." Lenard shifted his gaze and intensified his glare. Marvin's eyes expanded when he realized what he meant. "Oh hell no. Y-you can't make me do that!"

The sisters glanced back at Marvin with confused expressions before Alice turned to face Lenard. "What is he talking about?" She asked.

"That thing will get off our tail if we make Marvin go off on his own," He said. It would mean Marvin's ensured death, but he saw that as only fair after he tricked them.

"No…no. Please, I can help you fight off that thing. I know its weakness, if you bring me to your camp I can help you." He placed the palms of his hands together and bobbed them. "I have experience dealing with it. Besides, there's no guarantee that *The Nothingness* will follow me."

He made a valid point, Lenard thought. With no certainty that the monster will follow Marvin once he leaves, it would only make them more vulnerable. There was also the chance that Marvin might abandon them as soon as they reached camp.

If he did send Marvin to be a distraction, it would mean taking the life of another person. He may not be the one to kill Marvin, but he might as well be. Marvin might even be killed in vain. He took a deep breath in then exhaled. There had to be some way to bring Marvin, while also guaranteeing he would help them.

"We'll go with your plan," he sighed, "but, I *need* your promise that you'll help us. No running off." Marvin nodded as he approached Lenard and raised his hand.

They shook hands. The two of them stared deep into each other's eyes. Lenard did not see any sign that Marvin was lying. He released his hand. "So…do you have a plan exactly as to how to beat this thing?"

Hamon removed the bandages from his chest. The injury that lied there once had healed almost to completion. All they remained was a thin line of scabbing from the impact of the cut. Amber, who slept in the tent behind him, would disapprove of him removing the bandages so early.

He couldn't stand the lack of flexibility the bandages caused. The white material was now sullied with blood. He crumpled it up in a ball and tossed it into the fire behind him. Even with a lost sense of time, he could estimate it had been around a month since they began their journey. He hoped that the other members had not gone on the same endless path as they have.

The Forest had been growing stranger. The trees were marked with unfamiliar patterns. Some of the trees even had wood of a white color, opposed to the brown oak. They stumbled across many different unfamiliar objects.

Some of them Amber had claimed to recognize from the other world. He had no sense of what this place was, but he had a feeling it wasn't the same woods he typically ventured. This place felt distant, alien even. The pebble path had led them to another campsite. It still continued on past it as well.

The water he was drinking made him feel the urge to piss. He stood up and stepped to the edge of the camp. As he was about to get on with his business, a flick of fire illuminated an object in the distance for a brief moment.

His eyes caught a tiny glimpse of it. What got his attention was the contortion of light from glass the small flicker caused. That reflection stood at least fifteen feet in the air. He squinted his eyes as he leaned his face closer. The illumination from the fire grazed the structure just enough to be visible.

He turned back to the camp and leaned over Amber's tent. "Amber," he whispered. "Get up, there's something out there." The tent fabric shuffled before the zipper opened. Amber poked her head out and faced him. Hamon pointed at the direction of the structure. "I saw something over there." Amber flattened her brow and tightened her lips. He sighed, "Just come check it out with me." She sighed as she crawled out from the tent.

She stretched her arms. Hamon grabbed the torch from the ground and ignited it. He led her to the edge of the camp. The outline of the structure was more visible due to the extra light from the torch. There was a wall of oak planks, with a door in between two windows. Amber stepped in front of him.

"It's a house," She whispered. He furrowed his brow. "I've seen these from the other world. People would live in them. They're basically better versions of tents," She spun her hand.

A stone stairway led to the door. He placed his foot on the top step and lifted himself to the door. He grasped the circular handle with his free hand. It felt cold and metallic with small dents in the metal. The door creaked when he opened it. The floor was made of oak, a table sat a dozen feet away from the door. More glass at the back end distorted the light from the torch.

They walked further into the house. To the left was a ling chair of fabric. On the other side were two other tables. One was the same as the table in front of them, the other was a table that outlined the walls of that area.

"Do you have any idea what any of this is?" He asked.

"That over there," she pointed to the area to the right, "It's a…kitchen, and that," She brought her hand to the other side. "That's a living room." Further down the house was another pair of stairs, these ones leading to another level of the house.

"Up there, we should find a bedroom. It could be a good place to rest." He nodded as they scooched past the table and approached the stairs. They walked up the steps to the higher floor. The sensation of being in a higher area felt foreign to them. It caused a feeling as if the floor could cave in at any moment. On the second floor was a hallway filled with more doors.

Each door lined up with another on the opposite side, with one last door at the end of the hallway. They traveled to that door. The handle had the same cold feeling to it as the other. He opened it. A window sat on the wall in front of them.

The bonfire from the camp was visible from there. A bed rested against the wall of the left side of the room. A smaller table sat next to it. On the other side was a dresser. Amber rushed toward it and opened one of the drawers. She gasped as a wide smile consumed her face. She pulled out a brown t-shirt. He stepped next to her and glanced down into the drawer.

Clothes were stacked on top of each other. Fresh, clean looking clothes, as opposed to the ragged and torn clothing that he would find at campsites. He reached his hand within and pulled out a black t-shirt. The material was soft and comfortable.

He threw it on the bed behind him and pulled out another drawer above that one. This drawer contained jackets. The drawer below the one with shirts had jeans and soft pants. Amber stood up right, “Hold on.” She rushed out of the bedroom and out of sight. The echoes of a door opening traveled into the room.

He peeked his head down the hall. The door on the left closest to the bedroom was opened. There was a metallic screech as a loud pouring noise blared. “Yes!!” Amber shouted from in the room. Inside the room was a large, white, bowl type structure, with another table connected to the wall on the side. The floor was made of smooth, white tiles. Amber crouched outside of the large white bowl. A metal hose sat above it. Water poured into the bowl. She turned to face him.

"It's a bathtub!" An open smile plastered her face. "I remember these. People from the other world would use them to bathe. Oh…I wish Kaylee could see this." He had no clue what she was on about but smiled with her anyway. "You strip down and soak in water for a little while. I had small memories of these. It was one of the biggest things from the other world I wished we had."

Once the tub was halfway filled with water, Amber twisted a lever that stopped the water from flowing out of the metal hose. She stood up, "I'm going to go grab some clothes and try it out. You're welcome to give it a go after."

She stepped past him and out of the room. He turned to the door. A weird ashy smell hit his nose and caused him to cough. The smoke from the torch piled onto the ceiling. He patted out the flames, engulfing him in darkness. He reached for the lantern on his side as well as a lighter and lit the candle inside.

The new light illuminated the room. He placed the lantern on the table and walked out of the room. Amber met him in the hallway with a pair of clothes wrapped around her arms. "I've got the lantern set up in there," He pointed his thumb behind.

"Thanks," she said as she scooched past him and entered the tub room. She shut the door behind her. He came back to the bedroom. Its contents were still somewhat visible thanks to the bonfire outside the window.

He sat on the bed. The cotton blanket was fluffy and the pillows were soft. He almost fell asleep just lying on it. The muffled crackling from the fire created a soothing background noise.

He shut his eyes as his mind began to draft off. His weight became lighter and the noise became quieter. Amber's muffled humming from the bath could be heard. A bit of guilt laid on him. Lenard and the sisters were still out there. Maybe they did not deserve to be relaxing to such a degree, he thought. His concerns faded to the back of his head as he fell asleep.

Chapter 18

The Ceiling

The abyss appeared darker than before. Mark could not tell if it was because of the lack of sleep he had been getting. Many nights had past of him only being able to roll around in his blanket. Sleep was hard to get because of the feeling of vulnerability. Half their original members made for a poor defense. The few nights he did get rest, it always followed the same nightmare.

An Eldric creature slaughtered all of them in a blink of an eye. *The Forest* itself felt stranger than before. As if something could pop out from the abyss at any moment. The constant fear frustrated him. He had always been afraid, but now it felt so much more primal. Even a small snap of a twig caused by another member would be enough to make him flinch.

He sat crouched down beside the center fire. Across from it Klyde and Picc talked to each other. He had tuned out their conversation long before. In his hand he held an empty MRE. He threw the packet into the fire and watched it slowly burn. Behind him he could hear Quinton and Jarold working on the water mill.

There was another reason everything felt darker. No one had dared to say it yet, but he knew it was coming. Klyde…or maybe Picc, was going to announce that the search for their missing members is over, and they will be written off as deceased. A decision he did not want to come to pass.

He felt hopeless knowing there was nothing he could do to stop it. The truth he now held was that the other members were willing to let them go, to cut the search as a loss. They were tired of searching…tired of not finding anything…tired of holding out pointless hope.

He held a feeling of spite toward them, that they would give up on their own so easily. The truth was he was being unreasonable. These people are not Hamon, or even Lenard. They do not possess the same level of loyalty that those two do, not even Klyde.

Maybe he could, he swore he could. Even if it meant going through hell and back. Yet, here he sat, giving up like everyone else. Because of his fear. The unsettling fear of what lies in *The Forest*. If he had someone to go with him, surely he would search non-stop, he thought. He knew it was a pathetic excuse.

"Mark," Klyde called. He glanced up. Klyde stood with his arms crossed behind his back and with a firm posture. "Stop sitting around and go help on the water mill."

Mark gritted his teeth as his expression morphed into a glare. You're the one not doing anything, he thought in spite. He stood up and turned toward the artificial river. Quinton and Jarold sat around and did not appear to be doing much themselves.

Both of them only watched the water as it flowed. This irritated him even more. They were willing to sit around and do nothing, but not look for their missing members. He sighed as he leaned against the structure next to Quinton.

The two glanced at each other. Quinton shifted his body to be facing Mark, "You know, Klyde isn't going to be too happy seeing you leaning about."

"Klyde can kiss my ass." Quinton's eyes expanded at his remark. It was a bit out of the blue. A knee-jerk reaction to the frustration that had boiled up within him.

"So, you two don't seem to be getting along," Quinton noted.

"Can you blame me?" He gestured his forearm. "The asshole can't leave me alone for five goddamn minutes."

Quinton chuckled, "It's probably because he's desperate to get this flashlight done."

Mark scoffed, "Right." He leaned the back of his head against the structure and sighed. "When the hell did everything start going so wrong."

"When we started playing sides. Our group should have never argued against all of this in the first place," Quinton stated.

Mark sneered, "How the hell does that make any sense. Lenard went missing on an expedition Picc sent him on. If we weren't trying to make this stupid fucking flashlight we wouldn't be in this mess."

"This flashlight will help us on the next grand expedition," Quinton said.

"An expedition that got one of our members killed," Mark retorted.

"An expedition that you voted for, if memory serves me right," Quinton said.

"I voted for it because I knew damn well our group couldn't survive on the scraps we were finding. I would have never voted for this shit had I known it would result in this." He gestured his hands out to the entire camp. Quinton groaned as he turned back to face the flowing water. "Tsk," Mark scoffed.

He gazed off into a dark spot of *The Forest* between two illuminated trees. Lenard, the sisters, Hamon, Amber, they all had to be just beyond there. If he were only brave enough, he could venture *The Forest* on his own.

Although, that might not be the greatest idea. That is how Amber and Hamon got themselves lost. However, perhaps it did not matter if it was about finding the missing members. He was tired of the fear he felt. This could be his opportunity to overcome it.

He pushed himself off of the structure and faced the gap in the trees directly. Quinton said nothing to him. He walked forward toward the edge of the camp. His mind filled with doubts the closer he came. The sense of paranoia heightened. When he was halfway there, past the center fire and nearing the edge fire, a bead of sweat dripped down his forehead.

He then passed the edge fire. The light of that fire crept away from him. Noise from Klyde and Picc's discussion faded out until it was inaudible. His hands began twitching and his breaths became more shallow.

As he faced unending darkness, thoughts of monster's killing him and dragging him away popped in his head. Anything could snap out and kill him. No one would ever know. They would search for him too.

The light of the fire barely touched him now. He had to reassure himself with each step. Pellets of water formed in his eyes. His heart was racing so fast he thought it might burst out of his chest. He stopped and took deep breaths to calm himself.

The camp was far enough away that he could no longer be seen.

Lenard was capable of exploring out this far with no fear at all. How is it he could not do the same? Lenard also spent countless years in isolation. He could only imagine how frightened Lenard must have been. Yet, Lenard conquered that fear, he should be able to do it too.

He took another step forward. All his senses shouted at him to turn back. He closed his eyes and imagined a different scenario. A scenario where Lenard, Hamon, Amber and the sisters were back home. Where they were all happy again. There was no fighting, no disagreements.

A nice time where they all sat around the fire, laughing at the stories they tell each other. The senses that screamed at him to leave now dimmed. The fear of death vanished. When he opened his eyes again, he was so far out the edge campfire was only a bead.

Now even with his senses returned, he did not hold nearly as much fear toward *The Forest*. The sweat that seeped his skin began to run cold. He brought his hands to the side of his arms and shivered. A feat he thought he couldn't achieve. This may not accomplish much, but it's a start. He smiled as he walked back to camp.

Tensions between Lenard and Marvin were still high. Marvin had not apologized, but even if he did, Lenard doubted he could find the mercy to forgive him. The sisters had not spoken in a while either. It could be due to exhaustion, but he knew that was a bit of a delusion.

"Hey," Marvin called.

"What?" He glared at him.

"How did you know I was lying to you? Like…how did you figure it out?" Marvin asked.

"Reasons. Just be happy that I found out in the first place." He wondered if Marvin would even believe his story of seeing into the past through Picc's memories. It was quite the tale, and a hard one to believe. He himself did not know why he entered into these dream sequences. Why him? Why not someone smarter, like Hamon, or motivated, like Quinton. There had to be a reason for that.

What does it matter? He thought. The entire reason he wanted to see into those dream sequences in the first place was a dead end. He wondered why he was even surprised. He knows better than anyone that there is nothing for *The Forest* to give. So why did he grasp onto the dream sequences so much? Was it because it was what Kaylee would have done?

"How did you know?" Marvin asked again.

"I already told you."

"No, you didn't. I want to know how you figured it out," Marvin claimed.

"I don't have to tell you a damn thing," Lenard groaned.

"You were just threatening to toss me out to the monster. If I'm going to trust you I don't want any secrets between us, good friend," Marvin said.

Lenard turned to him and grabbed the collar of his shirt and pulled him closer. "You listen here. I figured it out because I could. Just because you want to help doesn't make me despise you any less. So if you don't keep your damn mouth shut I'll make that gash of yours worse."

Alice stepped in between them and made him let go of Marvin. "Break it up you two!" She demanded. Him and Marvin glared at each other.

"Whatever let's just keep going," he continued walking. Marvin and the sisters followed close behind. He took a deep breath in and sighed. When he turned back his gaze forward, he noticed a small bead of orange light in the distance. Another campsite.

One many they had stumbled upon during this long journey. He thought it might be a good idea to stop there. Get some rest. The problem was they were already behind schedule. Their three week trip had extended to a month. There was also the giant monster that could attack them at any time.

"There's a camp up ahead," He pointed toward the dot of fire. "Let's go take a quick rest there." He remembered they still needed to discuss how to beat *The Nothingness*. Marvin had only brushed him off each time he had asked. The others followed him to the fire. It was another typical campsite.

Two tents with a chest to the side of one. Six large rocks sat in a circle around the fire. Each one evenly spaced. He sat on the closest rock to their approach. The sisters decided to rest. Both of them entered the tent to his right. Marvin sat across from him. The flames of the fire sprouted high enough to obscure his face for brief moments.

"So…good friend. I have a suspicion you brought us here to discuss?" Marvin asked.

"Stop playing around it. How do we fight this…*The Nothingness*. I know you mentioned its weakness, but I'm guessing you have an actual plan in mind."

"Well, can you blame me for being so secretive. This information is all that is promising me life. How do I know you want to toss me to it once I spill the beans?"

Lenard arched an eyebrow, "Spill the?...whatever. You have my promise that I will not kill you. Trust me, I'm not the kind of man that wants that on my conscience."

"Nobody ever really does," Marvin shrugged. "But that doesn't stop people from killing anyway. I need something more, a trade of sorts."

Lenard clenched his fist and gritted his teeth, "You don't have the right to be demanding shit from us, not after your little stunt."

Marvin sighed as he leaned back, "Despite what you may think, my intention was never to get you killed." Lenard scoffed. He cleared his throat, "My intention was to get that thing off of me. Something that I should remind you, was your own fault. That's why I told you its weakness."

"Why the hell did you not just tell us to begin with!" Lenard yelled.

"Because I didn't trust you. I still don't. Sorry," he spread his arms. "That's just how it is. Now I'll tell you how to fight this thing, but you have to understand. That's not because I feel guilty, it's for my own survival. If I can't guarantee my own life, then I can't help you."

His warped sense of morality irritated Lenard. His smug voice he spoke with added to that. Nonetheless, he made a good point. There was nothing to be gained for him by telling them everything now.

He sighed, "What is it you want? It's not like we have much to give."

Marvin chuckled, "Oh, but you do. How did you figure out I was lying?" Lenard rolled his eyes and groaned as soon as the words left his mouth. "Information for information," He raised his hands toward Lenard. "It's only fair. I spoil my secrets, you spoil yours, good friend."

Would he even believe it if he told him? Lenard wondered. How should he even begin to do so? "Fine. A month and a half ago, some members and myself went on what we called the Grand Expedition. A five day long expedition. Sounds pathetic now, but it was big for us back then. During…the third night, I fell asleep. I had a dream, a weird dream. I was Picc…in your old group."

Marvin's eyebrows wrinkled and he scrunched his mouth, "What the hell are you on about?"

Lenard shrugged as he pursed his lips, "I have no idea myself. But I now know those memories were real…well I found out a while ago. Anyway, when I fainted, I went back into that dream sequence. While I was there, I got permission from your old captain to look at the monster log. I was trying to find more on *The Breathing From Above*. I found the page of *The Nothingness* right next to it."

He glanced at Marvin. He looked at him as if his head were on fire. Looks like he was right to think Marvin would not believe him. "I know it sounds almost impossible to believe, but I can prove it if you want," Lenard stated.

Marvin jolted from his rock, "Show me."

Lenard casted a smile as he waved his index finger at him, "Ah-ah, I told you how I found out, you never asked me to prove it. information for information, remember, good friend?"

Marvin sneered, "What else do you want to know?"

"Tell me how we are going to fight *The Nothingness*, first." Marvin nodded as he unwrapped his bag from his shoulders and unzipped the cover. He reached inside and pulled out a small, metal canister. A liquid swished around inside of it. Marvin tossed it over the fire to Lenard.

The canister had a black wrapper around it with a fire icon on the front. "It's gasoline. It's one of the items I found that I kept secret for myself. Sprinkle a little bit of that on anything, it will light ablaze for hours.

I injected some of the pellets of the musket with that, when I fired it that pellets would explode on impact. Dousing the blade of that katana I gave you should result in a badass fire sword."

"And you're positive this will be enough to kill it?" Lenard asked.

"I ain't sure of anything. But I know it will be a big damn help," Marvin claimed.

He nodded as he stored the gasoline in the side pocket of his bag. "Right. As for proof, your captain had a small hut he lived in. He was becoming desperate toward the end because he wanted his hands on that musket. You must have found that thing right around the time your campsite fell apart."

Marvin glanced at the musket that hung on the side of his bag, "I found it when I was running away. Ironic, I know. Now, what is it you wanted to know?"

"You're lying to me about *The Breathing From Above.* I know because in my first dream sequence, we came across it. You and your old outer woods expedition buddies. Tell me everything you know," Lenard demanded.

He sighed as his sight fell to the ground as he sat back down, "I know what you're talking about. I hate to say it, but if you saw the monster log page, then you know everything about it that I do."

"Bullshit! There has to be something more to it," Lenard claimed.

Marvin sighed, "There is one thing." He placed the hand on the back of his neck, "I didn't want to mention it because I thought it was pointless."

"What is it?"

He pursed his lip, "When I was younger, I heard a little tale from an older gentleman. I don't know why, the pal refused to tell me, but…they had a nickname for it."

Lenard leaned closer in his chair. "They called it *The Ceiling.*"

Mark sat in the back of the group. They huddled around the artificial river. Countless copper wires protruded from the mill. Picc sat at its feet. The copper wires fed into a metal cylinder Klyde had forged.

It was about to happen. The flashlight was about to become operational. A whole month's worth of work was about to pay off. So many possibilities were about to open up for them. Yet, he had only one thing on his mind he wished to use it for.

Klyde stood above Picc and was glancing down at him. Picc smiled as he plugged in the last of the copper wires. “Alright, only a couple minutes and this thing will be turned on.”

“How long will it last out of the mill?” Klyde asked.

Picc waved his hand, “An hour or two, give or take. It still needs some calibration. I have it set to sixty thousand lumens. It’s less like a flashlight and more like a stadium light from the other world. We should be able to see a couple miles.”

“That sounds a little too bright,” Klyde said.

Picc laughed as he nodded, “Exactly why it needs calibration. Once I test it out a bit more I should be able to ring it in a bit more. Just…don’t look directly at it.” Klyde dawned a concerned look.

Quinton leaned toward Mark, “Aren’t you excited?”

“Why should I be?” He asked.

“Why shouldn’t you be?” The flashlight would help with both his and Klyde’s goal. Still, something wasn’t right. He couldn't shake this sinking feeling in his stomach. Something bad was going to happen. Then, for a slight moment, he heard a noise. So short he couldn’t make it out as he heard it. He only processed the noise after it stopped. *Breathing*, and not the kind that sounded human. He glanced up. His gaze was met with darkness.

“Something wrong?” Quinton asked. He looked back down and shook his head.

"Why don't you give it a little test run? So we can see how it works." Jarold suggested. It was obvious how eager he was. A big smile plastered his face as he asked.

"I don't know. I don't want anyone accidentally going blind from this," Klyde said.

"A test drive should be fine. So long as I keep it pointed at the sky." Klyde sighed as he stepped further back. "Alright…Jarold, you're the one who suggested it. Give me a countdown."

He grinned as he held his hand up. "On three…one." He heard the breathing again, a deep raspy breath. It didn't go away this time.

"Two…"

He glanced upwards. The sound was so clear he was almost able to make out its figure.

"Three!"

The beam of light shined up. An accomplishment none of them had ever experienced. A feat made for celebration. Yet…they remained silent.

There was something else. Something none of them expected. The sight was so horrific it left them with their mouths gaped. They saw *something*. So far up it was hard to make out the details. As what Mark saw became clearer, his stomach sank with dread.

What they saw was flesh, writhing, shifting, bloody flesh. It extended in all directions beyond what the flashlight made visible to them. Small holes that had something hanging from it dotted the flesh. It was too far up to tell, but he swore what hung from those holes were human bodies. The flesh contorted as it breathed. The noise was now audible to everyone. It was a *ceiling*.

And it screeched.

Chapter 19

The Biggest Liar

A thin beam of light towered in the sky. It was so bright Lenard could see it even when it appeared to be a hundred feet away. Then, a loud screeching noise. The noise was so intense he instinctively raised his hands to his ears.

It sounded like a creature crying out. He groaned from the pain. Marvin and the sisters had their ears covered as well. What the hell was going on? He thought. What was causing such a loud noise? The screeching began to fade. The beam of light disappeared. His hands slinked down from his ears.

He heard Marvin breathing heavily beside him, "What the hell was that?" Marvin asked. A beam of light in the sky. That had to be Picc and his flashlight. But what made the screeching noise.

"I don't know. But I think it came from our camp! We need to get over there, now!" Lenard ordered. He jogged to the direction the light came from. As he heard the footsteps of the others catching up behind him, he picked up the pace. They ran for a while, longer than Lenard bothered to keep track of. Then he could see the three dots of light from their bonfires. They were almost home.

The voices of the others became audible. "We're here!" Lenard shouted. A smile crept on his face as he heart raced.

He could hear Alice and Jean's excited laughter behind him. A silhouette stood in front of the nearest fire. Two more followed. He was able to make out their details. A bulky but short man in the center, that had to be Mark. The other two had to be Quinton and Jarold..

"Lenard?!" Mark quivered as he ran to them as well. They met at the edge of the camp. Lenard and Mark collided in a hug. The sisters followed right after. Then Quinton and Jarold joined in. The entire group formed into one massive pile. Tears of joy streamed down Lenard's face. When he opened his eyes, he found that to be the same with everyone else. They were home.

Mark raised an MRE from the fire using the fire poker. He carefully placed the packet in his hand. The heat seeped into his hand before it faded to a mean temperature. Jean and Alice sat across from him on the ground with a blanket wrapped around them. Jean had already dug into an MRE.

Quinton and Jarold had gone back to the mill. Mark delivered the second one to Alice. She smiled at him as he handed it to her. Lenard and a man unknown to Mark stood a dozen feet behind the sisters.

Mark approached them. They turned to face him as he did so. "Hey, I'm Mark, who are you?" He asked the man.

The man smiled, "It's Marvin. It's a pleasure to meet you, good friend," Marvin shook his hand.

"Are you sure you guys don't want to come and eat?" Mark asked.

Lenard shook his head, "We don't have time. A monster is coming, a big one."

He raised his shoulders and wore a concerned face, "What are you talking about?"

"*The Nothingness*," Marvin interrupted. "A massive creature, bigger than you've ever seen. It will be here in a couple of hours at least. Where's Picc?"

"Uhh…he's…out. Him and Klyde rushed off to an expedition right before we heard your voices."

"Sounds like him," Lenard said. "What caused that screeching noise? And that beam of light, was that you?"

Mark raised his hands and his eyes squinted. "Just…hold on. There's too much going on right now. This monster. What the hell is it?"

Marvin shrugged, "Wish we could tell you. But not even I have a good idea."

"Okay…then…who are you, exactly?" Mark questioned.

Lenard gestured his hand at Marvin, "He's from Picc's old group. It's a long story, but he has a lot of tools at his disposal that will help us beat this thing. He also has a musket."

"You do?!" Marvin nodded with a proud smile on his face.

Lenard placed his hands on Mark's shoulders, "Now…I need you to listen to me. What was the screeching noise?"

His mouth gaped, "I…I don't know. It was…a ceiling. We saw it in the sky when we turned on the flashlight. We panicked for a second, then we heard your voices. Lenard's expression expanded.

His eyes fell from Mark's. "Where's Hamon…Amber as well, I haven't seen either of them."

"Hamon and Amber went out looking for you two. There's been no trace of them." He gulped as he tightened his grip on Mark's shoulders, "I need you to do something for me. You're not going to like it…but I need you to do it." Mark nodded. "I need you to take the sisters and get out of here. Go the opposite way we came from. We'll slow this thing down enough to get it off your tail."

Mark's gaze sharpened, "No…no! I just got you guys back…I'm not leaving without you!"

"You don't have a choice. If you don't…you and the sisters could be killed. The rest of us need to stay back and fight," Lenard said.

Mark swiped Lenard's arms from his shoulders, "No! You can't make me do this!"

"You have to....I'm sorry." Mark's sneer faded. His expression morphed into a face of dread. Lenard exhaled a quivered breath, "We'll get you packed up and ready to get you out of here in half an hour. Look after those two, keep them safe and out of harm's way."

Small pellets of water formed in Mark's eyes, "I-I…I can't. I'm not like you, or Hamon or Klyde. I can't go out there on my own."

"You won't be on your own, you'll have the sisters." Mark whipped a tear from his eye, then kept his hand rested on his forehead. "How about this?" Lenard smiled, "We'll kick that thing's ass, then I'll go find Hamon and Amber…we'll all make it back to you…we'll all be back together again. Sounds good, right?"

Mark chuckled, "I like that plan a lot better."

"I know you would. Now…I need you to grab three bags. Fill them to the brink with water canisters and MREs, as much as you can get. Grab all of our tools. It will be a lot of weight…I know, but I need you to keep going as long as you can. Don't turn back."

"I'll lay a pebble path…so you guys can follow after you beat the creature," Mark offered.

Lenard shook his head, "Don't…Marvin has a way he can find you…he has a map. So…no pebble path needed. Now, go get everything…Let Quinton and Jarold know as well." Mark nodded as he ran off. Lenard watched him grab the bags then turn to the chest. Lenard spun to Marvin.

"The map is only useful if we know what direction they're heading," Marvin said.

He breathed deeply, "I know…That wasn't the point." Marvin pursed his lips and he unwrapped his bag from his shoulders.

"Well then, we better at least make the act convincing. I think that's the least you could do, good friend," Marvin said with a smile.

Lenard smiled softly, "You have a point…good friend."

Hamon could no longer feel the scratch irritating his skin while he moved. It was almost healed. The new soft clothing he wore helped as well. Despite how long the two of them had been searching, it felt as if he was refreshed.

He wasn't tired, had clothes that weren't sullied in dirt and sweat and had freshened hair. His rest had been the best he had ever gotten. He almost felt…good.

He laid in the sheets of the bed near the campfire. His limbs spread across each corner of the bed. The soft blanket covered everything up to his neck. Amber slept in a different room. She opposed it at first, as she was paranoid something would happen to her. He gave her the lantern to sleep with to settle her worries.

As a trade, he got the room where the window faced the campfire. The crackling of the fire could still be somewhat heard. Amber shifting around in her bed was also audible. She had been moving around so much, he wondered if she managed to get any sleep at all.

He threw the covers off of himself, then stood up. The bed creaked. His bear feet smacked on the wood floor. The house shook a little when he landed. Amber must have heard him. Her door opened and her footsteps stopped right outside his door. A knock came shortly after.

"Are you up?" She asked.

"Yes," he said as he picked his bag off of the ground and swiped it over his shoulders. "Give me a second to grab everything."

Amber's weight pressed against the door. He stuck on his shoes, then grabbed a couple articles of clothing from the drawer. When he opened the door Amber stumbled over a little as she had not stopped leaning against it.

He smirked as she corrected her balance. She turned and glared at him. "Sleep well?" He asked with a smug face.

"I slept fine…thanks." She groaned.

"Well I slept like a baby. Best sleep I ever had," he laughed.

Amber rolled her eyes, "Whatever. Let's just get out of here, this place gives me the creeps." She crossed her arms and shivered.

"You have the lantern?" She nodded as she disappeared into her room for a second, then came out with the lantern in her hands.

"Are you going to use it? I thought we were sticking with the torch?" She asked.

Hamon sneered, "I hate hauling that thing around all the damn time."

"Oh come on, I thought you were supposed to be all big and strong." Amber grinned.

"Pfft, why don't you try carrying that thing for hours. Maybe I'll consider helping out once you start begging for it," He countered. Amber giggled. The house rattled for a brief moment. Small objects shook in place. Hamon and Amber silenced themselves as they glanced up.

"What was that?" Hamon asked.

"I…think it's just the house settling. I…I'm not sure," Amber laughed nervously.

He exhaled a calming breath, "Right…anyway, I'll use the torch…just to keep ourselves safe." Amber nodded. He took the lantern from Amber's hand and lit it. They walked down the stairs back to the center table then to the front door. He opened the door. The bonfire sat in direct view of them.

His leather boot collided against the stone of the bottom step of the stairway. The air outside felt noticeably less humid than inside. The transfer in temperature was intense enough to make him shiver. Amber exited the house behind him. He turned to see her stepping off of the stairway onto the grass beyond it.

From above, a shadow flickered in the corner of his eye. He glanced up at the left corner of the house. The shadows remained still aside from the spurts of fire. That must have been it, he thought.

"What is it?" Amber asked.

He rattled his head, "It's nothing, don't worry about it." A long, slimy tentacle appeared above Amber's head. His mouth gaped and eye's expanded, "Watch out!" He shouted. Amber turned around and saw the tentacle.

She moved out of the way just as it zipped down and pierced the ground where she stood. He wrapped his arm around her waist and moved her further back, then behind him. The tentacle dug itself out of the ground as he pulled out his dagger. It swiped at Hamon.

He ducked out of the way as it struck clean through the tree next to him. Amber pulled him away as the tree crashed down in front of him.

One swipe of that tentacle will slice him in half, he realized. The tentacle whipped up into the air then struck down at him. He held the dagger up and sliced through the tentacle. It retracted as a creature in the shadows made a deep growl.

A slimy claw dug into the side of the house. A blob creature half the size of the house crawled down into the light of the fire. It was an amalgamation of pink flesh and slime that walked on all fours. Its flaps of fat overlapped each other and its entire face dropped, with spike-like, brownish teeth. Several tentacles protruded from its back like tails.

It growled at him. They had to run. He could not possibly fight whatever the hell this was. Amber quivered next to him. She had tears forming in her eyes. She was in no condition to run, he had to fight. The creature thrusted several tentacles in their direction.

Hamon tackled Amber to the side as the tentacles pierced into the fire behind them. It cried in pain as it retracted its tentacles. He stood up but kept his hand pressed on Amber to keep her down.

Fire. That was its weakness. It may be an unfamiliar monster, but it's still a monster. He dove for the fire. The creature swung another one of its tentacles at him. He slashed it with his dagger.

He reached into the fire and grabbed an ignited piece of wood. It scorched his hand. The creature again thrusted several tentacles at him. He grit his teeth and swung the piece of wood at the tentacles. A few managed to make it past his counterattack and grazed his hip.

The rest were flung back as the monster cried in pain again. It screeched at him. Hamon ran toward the creature as it prepared to fling its tentacles at him again. The creature took a few steps back as it whipped its tentacles at him. He managed to dodge all but one that slashed his stomach.

He winced in pain as he clutched the gash but continued running toward the monster. More tentacles came flying at him as he dodged them. The tentacles then surrounded and flung in on him. He slid to the ground as the tentacles propelled over him.

His grip became looser on the wood as it burned through the skin on his fingers. The monster leaned toward him as it attempted to bite him. Hamon lodged his dagger in its eye before its teeth reached him. He shoved the piece of wood down the monster's throat. Its spike-like teeth clamped onto his arm and pierced clean through it. He screamed in pain.

"Hamon!" Amber shouted. He placed his foot on the monster's face as he ripped away from its jaw, his arm ripping off with it. The monster cried in pain as it coughed up blood and smoke.

Hamon wobbled as he watched the monster burn. It thrusted a tentacle at him in reflex in pain. He was too exhausted to move as the tentacle pierced his stomach. The force of the tentacle pushed him several feet onto his back. The monster screeched and shouted in pain, he then heard it run away. Its screams faded into the abyss.

The pain he felt was too great to feel any joy in surviving. Amber appeared above him with tears streaming down her eyes. He reached his right hand to her cheek. She held it as she sobbed.

Why was she so sad? He wondered. His senses grew delirious and his vision blurry. His hand fell to his stomach, where he felt the hole that now punctured him. Now he gets it…he was dying, he thought as his vision faded.

Lenard and Marvin sat together at the center fire with a large piece of paper in front of them. They were discussing battle strategies. In less than an hour, death would be knocking on their front door.

They had little time to plan and so much more to do. Lenard discussed with Quinton and Jarold about them staying back to help fight. They were reluctant but agreed. Now all that was left was to send Mark on his way. There was only one problem with that. Picc and Klyde still had not yet returned.

Lenard was sure Mark would not mind seeing Picc, but Klyde was a different story. He could not send Mark off without him saying goodbye to Klyde. There was also the layer of stress of having to explain the situation to the both of them. He was certain that Picc would want to leave with Mark.

He sighed. Marvin giggled to his side, "The end days do seem to be doing much for your mental health, good friend."

Lenard smirked, "I'll manage. It's not like this is the first time I've come face to face with death."

"Neither for any of us. Yet, this situation can't help but feel dreadful, am I right?" Marvin said.

He nodded, "I…I just wish I could see Hamon one last time before I go. I…I want to know if he's safe. I'm the whole reason Amber and him went out on their own anyway."

"Nope," Marvin shook his head. "That's not your fault. You shouldn't waste time blaming yourself for things you can't control good friend."

Then who's fault is it? Lenard wondered. Why did it feel like the world was coming to an end today? Mark will survive, the sisters as well. They'll start from anew. Marvin pulled a bottle of alcohol from his bag. Lenard now had extensive knowledge on it because of Marvin's ramblings he went on during their journey home. Marvin took a swig.

"Mind if I have a sip?" Lenard asked as Marvin turned to face him. "Good friend?" He added. Marvin grinned as he passed the bottle to him. He lifted the bottle to his mouth and took a large guzzle.

"Nothing like impending doom to make a drink taste sweet," He laughed. Lenard gritted his teeth as the bitter taste touched his tongue. His hand fell on his chest when the burning sensation kicked in.

Marvin shifted his gaze to behind him. He glanced back and saw Mark approaching him with a large bag strapped around his shoulders. He stood up from the ground and met Mark half-way. "What's going on? The sister's giving you trouble?"

Mark rocked his head, "No…I mean, they did but…they came around. How long do we have left?"

"Not long…If…If you feel you need to, then head out now," Lenard said.

"But…what about Klyde and Picc?" Mark asked.

Lenard faintly grunted, "I don't know if you'll have time to see them…I'm sorry. I can give Klyde your goodbyes for you, but…there's not much else we can do."

Mark's expression saddened, "Okay…Then we'll leave now. Let me go get the sisters." He turned around and jogged away. This was it…

"He seems like a good kid…I hope he makes it out there," Marvin said. Lenard turned to him as he took another gulp of alcohol.

Lenard exhaled, "I know he will. He doesn't act like it…but he's a tough one. I'm sure he and the sisters will be okay."

Marvin snickered, "Sound's like you aren't too sure of yourself. So long as he stays out of the outer woods like we discussed, he'll probably make it."

"Thank you for the reassurance, you bastard," he joked. Marvin grinned as he winked at him. After a couple minutes,

Mark came back around with the sisters behind him. Tears clouded their eyes and their hair was a mess.

"Sorry for taking so long, we wanted to say bye to you last." Mark was first, he let go of the sisters' hands and wrapped his arms around Lenard, "Thank you…for everything, even if you were a bit of a douche some times," Mark laughed with a shiver.

"Sometimes? I thought I was our camp's number one asshole?" He echoed Mark's hug. Mark and the sisters chuckled. Mark backed away after a couple seconds and stepped behind the sisters.

Alice was next, "Thank you…" she sobbed. "Thank you for getting us back home. Get back to us as soon as you can, okay!?" They hugged.

Jean was last, "You always used to act like an asshole, always reprimanding me for stuff. I may have been at fault for some of that. So…thanks, for always keeping me in line." One last hug. They regrouped and journeyed toward the edge of the camp. Lenard waved toward them as Mark lit the lantern and walked away. The dot of light from the lantern faded into the distance. He did not stop waving until it was out of view completely.

His legs gave out on him and he crouched to the ground. He sobbed. The tears he held back all came pouring out at once.

"Don't feel so sad, good friend. You did the right thing," Marvin said.

Lenard swallowed his tears and stood up and glanced back at him. Behind him Jarold and Quinton stood, tears running down their cheeks as well.

"Thanks, Marvin." Marvin smiled as he bobbed his head. Then, rustling came from another end of the camp. Lenard and the others glanced in the direction of the noise. A small fire hovering above the ground. It was Klyde and Picc. Lenard rushed to the edge of the camp.

Klyde came into view of the edge bonfire. The torch was in his hand. His expression widened when he saw Lenard approaching him.

"Lenard?" As soon as the words left his mouth Lenard wrapped his arms around him. "How are you alive?"

"How are you alive?" Picc echoed as he peered around Klyde.

"Sorry about that, you just have no idea how happy I am to see you. Now…this is going to sound like a lot, but I need you to listen because we don't have much time. There's a large monster coming for us, it will be here in less than an hour," He panted. Klyde raised his hands defensively. "We need to go over…battle strategies.

"Hold on…what are you talking about? How…how did you get back home? We all thought you were dead?" Lenard laid out his palms.

"Who are you?" A voice asked from behind. They all turned to face Marvin. He had an eyebrow arched and a sneer on his face.

"Marvin?" Picc asked. He stepped past Klyde and next to Lenard. "I…I can't believe you're alive." There was a hint of panic in his voice.

Marvin squinted his eyes, "Who are you?" He asked again.

"I-I-it's me…uhhh…you uhh…must not recognize me," he laughed nervously, "I mean, how many years has it been," he said while he spun his hand in the air.

"Lenard…what's going on? How did you make it back?" Klyde interrupted.

Lenard turned to face him, "Uhh…It was Marvin, he showed us the way back. He's from Picc's old group."

"Where's the sisters? Did they make it back with you? And where's Mark?" Lenard hesitated to answer the question. Not due to what the answer was, but because of how it was asked. Klyde sounded as if he held not even a single bit of concern in his voice, only caution.

"This isn't Picc," Marvin snickered while bobbing his index finger at him.

"What do you mean?"

Picc gestured his arms in the air, "I have no utter idea what he's talking about," he pointed at Marvin. That same nervous smile still plastered his face.

"I know who you are…You're that one kid…the creepy one. What the hell are you doing pretending to be Picc," Marvin said as he rushed toward him. Lenard blocked his path with his arm. Picc took a few steps back, almost tumbling backward.

"Marvin. You need to tell me what's going on? What do you mean that's not Picc," Lenard said.

"It's exactly what I said. That's not Picc!" He sneered.

"I am Picc! You have to believe me. I don't know why Marvin is acting so irrational." Marvin groaned as he shouted at Picc. Lenard shifted his weight to be pressing all of it against him.

Picc shouted back. They talked over each other so much Lenard was no longer able to make out what either of them were saying. He kept shouting at Marvin to calm down. Then, the barrel of the pistol appeared next to his face, only a couple feet away.

It pointed at Marvin's head. Lenard's eyes slowly traveled down the barrel, to Klyde's hand that gripped the handle. His first immediate thought was why Klyde had the gun pointed at him. Then he saw his face.

A grin of pure evil rested on it. It all made sense now. Why Klyde was so lenient with Picc, why he had been so distant, why his question felt so strange. This was *not* Klyde.

A bright flash of light and a loud bang ruptured Lenard's senses and caused to step backward. When his senses returned, the first thing he noticed was the blood that sprayed onto his arm. Then he looked to the ground.

Marvin's corpse laid in front, blood poured from the new hole in his head. Lenard faced Klyde again. The evil grin had vanished, now replaced with an expression of complete apathy.

Lenard screamed in anger as he tackled Klyde to the ground. He laid several punches to his face before Quinton dragged him away. Jarold stood on top of Klyde and kept him pinned down.

His breaths grew shallow and more frequent. The face of apathy didn't disappear from Klyde's face, nor did his punches leave a single mark. What the hell is that? Lenard thought. What the hell is going on?!

Chapter 20

A Call From The Abyss

Amber hovered above Hamon. He was placed against a tree by Amber. She desperately attempted to cover his wounds with bandages. Tears rolled down her eyes as she kept replacing the bandages that overflowed with blood.

Hamon sat with his mouth gaped and his eyes closed, barely responsive and growing more so by the minute. So much blood…there was so much blood. It overwhelmed her. She couldn't keep up. Each time she would replace a bandage another one would be soaking red with blood.

He wasn't going to make it. A reality she tried to keep pushed down but was failing to do so as Hamon's condition became worse.

"Don't leave me…Don't leave me alone here," she sobbed. She finished replacing the bandage on his missing arm and reached down to grab another. However, there wasn't another. There were no more bandages left. She clutched her thighs as she whispered 'no' to herself again and again.

Hamon's hand fell on her shoulder. He used what strength he had left to open his eyes. "It's going to be okay," he uttered. "Can…can you tell me…it's going to be okay?" She stared at him for a long moment.

She then swallowed her tears as she laid her hands on his shoulders, "You're going to be okay. You're going to be okay," she echoed. Hamon's eyes fell closed again as he leaned his head back. "We'll find Lenard and the sisters and go back home," she consoled him.

"I'll…say hi…to…Kaylee…for…you," He muttered.

With all her strength, she mustered a smile, "Thank you." Hamon's body remained still for a long time. Then, his breathing stopped and his muscles went limp. She stared at his corpse for god knows how long. It was long enough that his skin grew pale. His corpse…it reminded her of a memory she had forgotten.

One of her glimpses of the other world. People sat around her, wearing fancy, black suits. A red carpet led to a casket. A corpse she recognized but had no memory of lied within it. An older man with a receding hairline. A memory she had felt sorrow toward each time she remembered it. As if there was some reason she should remember the man.

She stood up, her legs wobbled so much she almost tripped doing so. She was on her own now. What should she do? Should she head back. That would be the logical thing to do. As she walked in the opposite direction she traversed the pebble path from, something called to her.

Not a voice, but a feeling. There was something to be found out at the end of this path…she needed to keep going. She turned around and grabbed the lantern from Hamon's corpse.

The light was obscured due to the blood that splattered across the glass. It was enough to allow her to see the way forward, and that was all she needed. She lit the lantern and continued down the pebble path.

Lenard sat in front of Klyde, who was now tied to the tree with several leather straps. Quinton and Jarold stood behind him. Any minute now they could be met with the most terrifying creature they will have ever faced. Now, they had another issue. The *thing* that sat before them. The blood from Marvin splattered across *The Thing's* face.

"What are you?" Lenard finally asked.

"What do you mean? I'm Klyde," it answered.

Lenard sneered, "Don't be coy with us. It doesn't matter what you say, you're not getting out of this."

It sighed and shifted its face toward the ground. Then *The Thing* laughed, "I suppose there is no point in hiding anything from you. It won't matter anymore." Its evil grin returned. "You're right, I'm not Klyde."

Lenard sheathed his katana and raised it to *The Thing's* neck, "Then what the hell are you?"

"I…don't know what you would call me. To be honest this is the first time I've ever been caught. For centuries I've been digging myself in groups. I don't possess any special abilities like my brothers do…so I have to handle things the hard way," It said.

"Your brothers?" Jarold questioned.

"Yes, the other creatures in this forest, the ones that have been hunting you down since you began breathing," it claimed.

"Is *The Ceiling* one of your brothers?" Lenard asked.

The creature chuckled, "No…but I can see how you would think that. He's…more like our father."

"And what does that thing want with us?" Lenard asked.

The Thing's grin grew wider, almost as if it were giddy, "You'll see soon enough."

Lenard rammed the katana into *The Thing's* shoulder, "How long have you been pretending to be Klyde?"

The creature laughed as green blood washed over the red. "Since you brought Picc here. I was following him, with the intent to slow him down enough so another monster could kill him. Then you people got to him first and led me to a treasure trove of new people to hunt." That long? Klyde had been taken from them for that long, and they didn't notice?

Lenard drew his katana and flicked the blood off of it. He stood up and walked past Quinton and Jarold, "We can't spend any more time on this, we need to get prepared."

"What should we do about fake Klyde?" Quinton asked.

"I…I don't know. Just killing it doesn't sound like a good enough punishment." Lenard approached his bag and grabbed the gasoline canister from the side pocket. "Let's just focus on dealing with *The Nothingness* for now." Quinton and Jarold nodded. He noticed their empty gazes. The confirmation of Klyde's death must be getting to them, he figured. He was upset as well, but he had dealt with death like this before.

"Quinton, take Marvin's musket. Jarold, keep the pistol," Jarold had taken it from Klyde when he tackled him. He nodded. Lenard opened the canister and carefully poured the liquid onto the blade of the katana.

Once it was covered, he closed the canister and stuck the blade into the bonfire in front of him. The flame traveled up the blade, igniting the katana. He raised it up. Marvin was right, this was pretty badass. Quinton had returned with the bloodied musket in hand.

Lenard staked his katana into the fire, "Can I see the baggie?" Quinton nodded as he pulled the plastic bag from his waist pocket. He placed it in Lenard's hand. Marvin mentioned something about injecting these with gasoline, maybe he could do that, Lenard thought.

The pellets had tiny holes that seeped into its hollow innings. It was too small to pour the gasoline. "Go bring Marvin's bag to me, please." Quinton nodded again as he wandered off.

"It's all a waste of time. You aren't going to kill *The Nothingness*," Lenard thought he heard *The Thing* speak.

When he turned he was met with Picc instead. Picc wore an exhausted expression. He wondered if it was because of Marvin's death. "That's not what I'm trying to accomplish. If I can hold this thing back long enough to keep Mark and the sisters safe, then I don't give a damn what happens to us." He then arched an eyebrow, "How do you know about *The Nothingness* anyway?"

Picc smirked as he stepped next to him, "Back in my old group, I would sneak into our captain's lodge in order to see our monster log…I was very curious about it. So I know quite a bit about it."

"You can remember something like that from that long ago?" Lenard questioned.

"I have a photographic memory. I remember everything," Picc said. Quinton returned with Marvin's bag in his hand and placed it next to him.

He turned from Picc to the bag and unzippered it. The bag was littered with tons of different utilities, bottles, MREs and a pack of smokes Marvin must have been saving.

Some of the utilities he recognized from the item log. Books, cups, nail clippers, but there was one item he was looking for. A syringe. He grabbed it and took it out of the bag. It was a glass syringe that fit in the palm of his hand.

He reopened the canister and stuck the needle inside. Gasoline filled the glass tube. Then, he took the needle out and placed the canister on the ground. The needle fit perfectly with the small hole of the pellet.

"Thanks, you can take the bag back now," Lenard ordered. Quinton grabbed it and hurried off.

"That's quite the idea. I'm surprised you managed to find that out on your own," Picc attempted to compliment him, but his smug voice made it sound more like an insult.

"Marvin talked about it when we were traveling back home," Lenard explained.

Picc chuckled, "That's how Marvin always was…he could never shut up about anything. I would ask him the simplest question and he would go on and on about it for hours."

Lenard snickered as he injected another pellet with gasoline. "Then tell me, why didn't he recognize you?"

"I don't know," Picc answered. Lenard turned to face him. He was hiding something, the way his eyes looked, Lenard could tell.

"He seemed pretty adamant about it. I don't think it was a case of him just not recognizing you." Lenard was able to recognize Marvin right away after an even greater amount of time. Picc had known him longer, there's something more to this, he knew it. "Be honest with me…are you really Picc?"

The two of them stared at each other. "I am. I haven't a clue as to why he didn't recognize me."

Lenard adjusted his gaze back to the pellets and injected another one. "Well, you have my condolences."

"Thank you, I appreciate that," Picc expressed.

"So…are you going to stay here and help us fight?" Lenard asked.

Picc shrugged, "I don't think I have a choice. It's too late to run from that thing."

"Good, then can I trust you to use the musket?" Lenard questioned.

Picc's expression widened slightly, "You are trusting me with something? I didn't expect that from you."

Lenard sneered, "Just because I am doesn't mean I trust you. It's that you are the only one here who really knows how to use it." If he could leave it in anyone else's hands, he would, he thought to himself.

Picc also had experience with *The Nothingness*. It made nothing but complete sense to leave their most powerful weapon in his hands.

"I suppose I could do that." Lenard finished injecting the last of the pellets and placed them all back into the baggie. He tossed it to Picc, who caught it, "Then don't let us down." As Picc nodded, The *Thing* behind him began to laugh.

They both shifted to look at him. "It's here," It cackled. Picc and Lenard turned toward the abyss. A large creature towered above the trees a couple dozen feet away from their camp. Its true size was like nothing Lenard could imagine.

He ducked for the musket and tossed it to Picc. "Get ready!" He shouted as he retrieved the katana from the bonfire. Quinton and Jarold rushed to him as the creature approached. The thud of its legs against the ground grew louder. Quiton held a sword, Jarold had the pistol.

They held their weapons out ready to attack, "Picc…when it reaches the bonfire, shoot it!" Lenard ordered.

"Alright," Picc nodded as he loaded the musket and raised it to the creature. It had so many red glowing eyes, too many to count. It had several legs that angled up and then hooked to the ground. It touched a singular leg into the light of the bonfire.

The force of it was so strong it tore the ground beneath it. The leg itself dimmed the light around it, almost as if it were radiating darkness. It was like staring at nothingness itself. When it leaned closer, Picc pulled the trigger on the musket. The pellet zoomed at the monster's heads and exploded on impact. The monster screeched as its movement paused.

"Fire another!" Lenard shouted. Picc reloaded the gun and fired at the monster again. Another explosion hit its face. The monster shrugged off the explosion as another one of its legs entered the light.

"Again!" Picc fired. The pellet hit dead on. More of its legs entered the camp. It was becoming clear that even the musket was not enough to damage this monster. Below its amalgamation of heads and red eyes were large, sharp fangs. Its mouth was not visible but must have lied somewhere there.

"Aim for the fangs!" Lenard shouted. Picc adjusted his aim and shot right in between its fangs. Its scream was much louder and it fell back a few steps. "Keep firing at that exact spot!" Lenard shouted as he took off from them.

"Where are you going!" Quinton shouted.

"Do go fight this thing up close!" Another explosion hit the monster as he reached it. He waited for it to stop moving its legs, then used his katana to slash the nearest leg to his left. The blade dug halfway into the monster's thick leg.

Lenard tried to pull the blade out, but it was lodged. Picc fired at the monster again, causing it to lose balance. The leg Lenard's katana was lodged into shifted backwards. The katana was pulled out, but Lenard fell onto his back due to the force.

A leg in the air was about to crash right on top of him. He rolled out of the way as the leg destroyed the ground beside him. Lenard stood up and laid a vertical slash into the leg. This monster did not bleed. No green ooze poured from the gash in its leg.

Lenard wondered if this thing could even be killed. He laid another slash as another explosive pellet hit the monster's mouth. The slashes were doing damage, but no more damage than the katana would output without the fire. There had to be something more when Marvin said fire was this thing's weakness.

More legs fell toward Lenard, he attempted to dodge them but one grazed his hip and caused him to bleed. Another explosion. One of its legs fell backward and struck Learned from behind. As he pulled himself up, the monster brought one of its legs above him and thrust it into the ground.

As the dust of the ground disappeared, Lenard saw Quinton helping him to his feet. "Thank you," Lenard said.

"Thank me later, let's just focus on killing this hell spawn." Lenard nodded as he grabbed the katana off the ground. The two of them whaled many strikes into one of the monster's legs. It caused enough pain to retract the leg back.

Lenard ran toward it and gave it a running strike. It was enough to slice a three foot portion of the monster's leg off. It screeched as it retracted its leg above to its body. One leg down, over a dozen left to go.

This beast had to have some sort of weak spot, an area where fire damage was more effective. Two explosions struck the monster's mouth this time. The force was so strong it knocked it back a dozen feet. No…they can win this, Lenard told himself.

Him and Quinton laid many strikes into another leg. Lenard managed to slice off a portion again before the monster retracted it. Jarold and Picc shot two more pellets at the monster. The explosion tore off its fang. They could do this…they could really do this! Just a bit more effort, and they could kill this thing. He could see Mark, and the sisters again…maybe even Hamon.

Lenard and Quinton split off, each taking their own leg and laying slashes into it. Before Lenard could finish off the leg, it was raised into the air. The monster lifted the leg above Quinton. He was too busy striking another leg to notice.

"Quinton!" Lenard called out as he sprinted toward him. It was too late, the monster thrusted its leg down upon Quinton. The force was so great all he saw was a puff of pink mist.

The sound of his bones crunching was still audible over the loud thud of the monster's leg that collided with the dirt. The monster lifted its leg from the ground, blood dripped from it. A small crater with blood splattered around it in every direction remained.

The sight caused Lenard to trip backward over his own leg. Another one of the monster's legs came crashing down in front of him as he lifted his head. He placed his hands on the ground behind him and pushed himself back. Blood followed him. He did not know why until he attempted to stand. The monster's leg did not fall in front of him, it fell on his legs. His legs were gone.

His breathing grew fast and shallow. Another round of explosions struck the creature. Lenard gritted his teeth as reached for the katana and crawled away.

He managed to avoid the monster's legs falling all around him as more rounds of explosions struck the creature. As he made it halfway to them, Jarold reached him and pulled him away from the monster. A trail of blood was left the entire way.

Jarold released him at the edge bonfire where Picc continued to fire more rounds. "What do we do now?" Jarold asked.

Lenard raised his hand to his forehead as a migraine set in, "I don't know…Marvin said fire is this thing's weakness…but it doesn't seem to be doing a damn thing!" His head was going fuzzy and he was close to losing consciousness.

He remembered when Marvin referred to this thing as 'the same as any other monster.' What the hell was he on about! This monster is faster, stronger, bigger and far more tankier.

There was just one way Lenard could think of this beat this thing. Somehow getting the fire inside of it. An idea popped into his head.

Another round of explosions struck the monster.

"Uhh...Lenard, there's a problem," Picc announced.

"What is it?" Lenard asked.

Picc held up a now empty baggie, "Were out of pellets."

This was perfect. "Okay...let the monster get close. I have an idea," he groaned. The monster shrugged off the smoke of the last explosion. Lenard ripped off a piece of his jacket and pulled out the gasoline canister.

He took a lighter out of his pocket, stuffed the cloth into the canister and lit the cloth. A contraption he was able to make due to the item log he got a brief glance at. *The Nothingness* approached them.

"Picc!" Lenard turned his head to look at him. "I need you to throw something at its eye when it gets close." Picc nodded as he grabbed a hatchet that laid on the ground. The monster towered over them. Its singular fang dangled above him. Picc aimed the hatchet at the monster.

"Throw it now!" Picc leaned his arm back then threw the hatchet with the force of his body. The hatchet flung straight into the monster's eye and pierced it. The creature screeched. When it opened its mouth Lenard threw the gasoline canister into it. The light of the flame vanished into the creature's throat.

A fiery explosion lit from the monster's mouth. Its wailing grew louder, almost ear piercing. It fell back and tumbled, then fell over its own weight. The force of its boding crashing into the ground was enough to shake the entire forest around them. It tried to pick itself back up but failed as the fire spread across its insides.

Lenard gazed upon the creature as he watched it slowly die. They did it, they managed to kill the beast. It let out its final gasps of air as whiffs of smoke puffed out from its mouth. Its massive corpse covered almost the entire campsite.

"Is it dead?" Jarold asked.

"I think…so," A large groan exhaled Lenard's throat. The boost in senses from the fight had worn off and the pain set in. Jarold rushed to his aid with bandages he had stored on him. He lifted each of Lenard's stubs and wrapped them. "Thanks," Lenard expressed.

"Don't mention it," Jarold tightened the last bandage and stood up. "So…if that things dead, now what?" Good question, Lenard thought. The reasonable thing to do is to find wherever Hamon and Amber went off to, or at least join Mark and the sisters.

"Let's just take it easy for right now. We'll need to find a way to get me moving again anyway," Lenard said.

"You know…There are these things from the other world called wheelchairs, they were used for people who couldn't walk. It shouldn't take us too long to make you one," Picc smiled at him.

He smiled back. "Thank yo-" he froze as a chill went down his spine. Several white dotted eyes peered through the abyss on the other side of the camp. Their fight with *The Nothingness* must have attracted them.

The Thing from behind them began to laugh, "You people don't understand the first thing about our kind." Several monsters peered through the abyss wall into the light of the fire. It was the normal monsters, but there were so many of them. Even if they were all in top condition they couldn't take down all of them.

Lenard noticed Picc's breathing growing frantic beside him, so he glanced at him. "I'm sorry…I'm sorry Lenard," he whispered as he took a couple steps back.

"No! Stay here! We can think of a plan!" He shouted. Picc did not listen as he turned around and ran. He disappeared into the void behind them. "Picc! Come back!!" Lenard shouted as his voice echoed into nothing. The monsters approached closer.

"What do we do?" Jarold asked with a quiver in his voice. Before Lenard could, a monster tackled Jarold to the ground and tore into him with its sharp claws. Bits of flash and guts flew off with each swipe. Lenard looked in horror as his friend died. Another monster stood above him and raised its claw.

This can't be how it ends! He screamed to himself. There had to be a way out! Its claw dashed to his chest where the sharp claws pierced him. The monster retracted its claw from his chest as blood spattered out from it.

As blood puddled around him his vision began to go blurry. The sound of the monster digging its claws into his flesh muffled as his senses went numb. As it all went black, he had a vision. A warm field of green grass, and a bright sun in the sky.

Sweat dripped down Picc's forehead as he ran. His breath was short and his balance tumbled. He held his arms in front of him to watch for trees that may lay in front of him. This feeling of exhaustion couldn't help but remind him of the first time he ran.

A monster's footsteps followed behind him and was fast approaching. He ignored the swelling in his chest and the cramps in his abs. He just needed to keep going, a little farther…and he would be safe.

The monster's footsteps reached next to him as he heard the sound of the beast swiping its claws. He ducked as the claw sliced a tree next to him clean in half. His ankle twisted as he picked himself up.

A grunt left his mouth with each sprint he took. A little farther…he could find a bonfire. Then, fate granted his wish, a bead of orange light in the distance. He ran toward it, with the monster right behind him.

"Please," he whispered to himself. His desperation for survival grew deeper. Then, the light of the fire disappeared. His body had gone limp as he lost touch with all his surroundings.

The change in pressure…he had fallen. He collided with the stone below.

The thud was so loud it echoed out of the chamber and into *The Forest.* Sharp pains littered his body. Many of his bones were broken. To his luck, the footsteps of the monster did not follow him downward. His leg was broken, and he was unable to stand. He was trapped down there.

A sense of panic rushed to his veins as he realized his dire situation. No food, no water and no way to get out…he was going to die here. "Hello!" His voice echoed up the chamber. "Anyone!!" He shouted.

"PLEASE HELP ME!!!" The scream was so loud and desperate he began to cough.

"HELP ME!!!" His voice faded. As he was about to shout again, someone faintly shushing him came from the dark catacombs. Picc focused his gaze on the shushing noise. It was too dark to see anything, but he swore he could make out the figure of a man.

His suspicion was confirmed when a fire was lit in the center of the man. The fire was stored in a metal container placed where the man's heart should be. A metal ring outlined his head and he wore a steampunk coat.

"Be quiet now…my child," He whispered in a chilling yet calming manner. His voice was raspy and mechanical.

"Who are you?" Picc uttered with his eyes wide.

The man smiled. "I am the one who will take you home. You suffered enough now child, come with me," The man held out his hand. The man had a warm glow to him, as if he were someone to be trusted. It was unnatural, almost as if his kind gesture was a lie.

Picc reached out his hand toward the man, "What's your name?" The man grasped onto his hand. His pain and injury dissipated like it was never there to begin with.

"I am the father," He answered as he carried Picc away.

The sky was brighter. Amber knew it for sure now. It was no longer pitch black, but more of a navy blue, perhaps even brighter than that. It was hard to tell with her senses being as dulled as they were. She had been walking nonstop for no less than three days, maybe even longer. No food, no sleep, no water. The voice she had in her head telling her to reach the end of the pebble path was all that kept her going.

She was in a half-dream state. Entire chunks of time spent walking would disappear from her memory. Those lost memories were replaced by ones of the other world. Even memories she never had before. As if she was growing closer to the other world.

A dream about her, Kaylee and Klyde. They lived in a nice house on the countryside. She would wake up each morning and make breakfast for them. Then she would see her husband off to work, then her daughter off to school. It was her favorite dream.

She then stumbled upon something she couldn't quite tell if was reality or dream. She reached the end of *The Forest.* The oak trees stopped at a cliffside standing above a beach. The harsh shadow of *The Forest* ended, and an earth illuminated by a sun sat in front of her.

The pebble path continued onward to the beach. She reached her hand out and the tip of her fingers reached the sun's illumination. Her whole body became consumed by the light. A warm feeling overcame her body. The turmoil and pain she felt faded.

She continued down the pebble path from the cliffside to the beach. The sand was soft and warm, as she always thought it would be in her dreams. The pebble path swirled across the beach's uneven ground to a small boat that rested on the edge of the shore.

Beyond the shore was blue water as far as the eye could see. Amber gazed down the horizon, she swore she could hear the voices of her loved ones calling to her. Kaylee, Hamon, Lenard, Klyde, even Quiton and Jarold. She stepped onto the small boat and grabbed the two pedals to her side. She steered the boat off the shore and into the ocean.

As she went farther, the voices grew louder. They told her to come over and be with them. She gazed back at *The Forest*. A massive disk of flesh hovered above it. Its rim stretched from each side farther than she could see.

Its flesh curved to the center like a cone, with tentacles stretching hundreds of meters into the sky. She took her gaze off of it and back toward the ocean.

A sense of peace came over her like she had won a horrible battle. She ventured out from one abyss to another. From a forest to an ocean. From one world…to the next. The unknown awaited her.

The End.

Author's Page

About The Author:

My name is Nathan Trull. I am an aspiring author and I hope to get my thoughts and ideas out into the world. Ever since I was little, coming up with different ideas for stories was something that I would always do. Whether it'd be an idea for the next big superhero film or some cool fantasy world, I had that sort of spark. As I got older, that spark never went away. My ambition to get my stories out into the world only grew. People would like to tell me it was because of my autism, I thought it was just a part of who I am.

I wasn't set on this path at first. I had expectations placed on me that weren't exactly set on what I wanted for myself at first. However, when I decided I wanted to be a writer my parents became more supportive of me. I chose to be a writer because it was the easiest to get into and something I could start at any time.

Now, after lots of dedication I have released my first book. It feels incredible to get an idea from my head onto something that others can experience for themselves. I can't wait to get more of my ideas out there. I hope that you can't wait to experience those ideas.

Made in the USA
Monee, IL
16 February 2025

12383618R00164